D1007066

How *to* Know You're Going *to* HEAVEN

JOHN ANKERBERG
JOHN WELDON

HARVEST HOUSE PUBLISHERS
EUGENE, OREGON

All Scripture quotations, unless otherwise indicated, are taken from the Holy Bible, New International Version®, NIV®. Copyright © 1973, 1978, 1984, 2011 by Biblica, Inc.® Used by permission. All rights reserved worldwide.

Verses marked NKJV are taken from the New King James Version®. Copyright © 1982 by Thomas Nelson, Inc. Used by permission. All rights reserved.

Verses marked NASB are taken from the New American Standard Bible®, © 1960, 1962, 1963, 1968, 1971, 1972, 1973, 1975, 1977, 1995 by The Lockman Foundation. Used by permission. (www.Lockman.org)

Verses marked (NLT) are taken from the Holy Bible, New Living Translation, copyright © 1996, 2004, 2007 by Tyndale House Foundation. Used by permission of Tyndale House Publishers, Inc., Carol Stream, Illinois 60188. All rights reserved.

Verses marked ESV are from The ESV® Bible (The Holy Bible, English Standard Version®), copyright © 2001 by Crossway, a publishing ministry of Good News Publishers. Used by permission. All rights reserved.

Verses marked KJV are taken from the King James Version of the Bible.

Italics in Scripture quotations indicate authors' emphasis.

Cover by Koechel Peterson & Associates, Inc., Minneapolis, Minnesota

Cover photo © Logray-2008 / iStock / Thinkstock

HOW TO KNOW YOU'RE GOING TO HEAVEN
Copyright © 2014 by The John Ankerberg Show
Published by Harvest House Publishers
Eugene, Oregon 97402
www.harvesthousepublishers.com

Library of Congress Cataloging-in-Publication Data
　Ankerberg, John, 1945-
　How to know you're going to heaven / John Ankerberg and John Weldon.
　　pages cm
　Includes bibliographical references.
　ISBN 978-0-7369-5942-1 (pbk.)
　ISBN 978-0-7369-5943-8 (eBook)
　1. Assurance (Theology) 2. Future life—Christianity. 3. Heaven—Christianity. 4. Salvation—Christianity. I. Title.
　BT785.A55 2014
　234—dc23

　　　　　　　　　　　　　　　　　　　　　　　　　　　2013043585

All rights reserved. No part of this publication may be reproduced, stored in a retrieval system, or transmitted in any form or by any means—electronic, mechanical, digital, photocopy, recording, or any other—except for brief quotations in printed reviews, without the prior permission of the publisher.

Printed in the United States of America
　　　14 15 16 17 18 19 20 21 22 / VP-JH / 10 9 8 7 6 5 4 3 2 1

Contents

Dedication

This book couldn't possibly be dedicated to anyone other than "the Lord our righteousness" (Jeremiah 23:6 kjv)—Jesus, the prophesied Messiah, our Lord and God incarnate—who at incalculable cost to Himself provided eternal redemption as an unreservedly free gift to all who would trust in Him and His finished work on Calvary: *Tetelestai*! (It is finished, paid in full!)

Yes, Lord, we "will praise you forever…for what you have done" (Psalm 52:9 nlt). "Not to us, Lord, not to us but to your name be the glory, because of your love and faithfulness" (Psalm 115:1).

Coauthor John Weldon would like to express his sincere gratitude to those who made the production of this book possible: Hal and JoLynn Lindsey, Betty and Kate Timson, Craig Branch, Fred and Jani Russell, Mike and Beth Charbonnet, Jacob Prasch, Mike Dosh, Charles Adams, MD, Ellen and Gloria, Crystal, Michelle, Shonda, Marsha, Cathy, Chrissy, and the remaining staff of the Full Circle Medical Center, Jennifer, Hillary and Helen, John and Darlene Ankerberg, Dillon Burroughs, Cathy Sims, Beth Lamberson, and David and Kelton for their encouragement through endurance in much suffering.

"What I long for, and what I think every person longs for, is the knowledge that my relationship with God is secure—permanently secure—not just for today, but for tomorrow and for all of eternity." [1]

—ERWIN W. LUTZER

Where Will You Spend Eternity?

This book is about the most important topic of your life—where you will spend eternity.

If you are a Christian, you can have full confidence you will go to heaven when you die. If you're not a believer in Jesus Christ or are uncertain, you'll read how to be certain and how you can dwell in heaven forever.

This teaching that the believer in Jesus Christ is saved forever is also called the doctrine of eternal security. Every Christian has doubts about their salvation at some point, a natural consequence of our sin nature interacting with a fallen world. But a look at God's Word, the Bible, provides ample evidence of the believer's eternally changed condition.

This book won't prevent the devil's attempts to make you doubt. But we hope that it will go a long way toward increasing your assurance so that you have no doubts as to your eternal destiny and, as a result, will "rejoice with joy inexpressible and full of glory" (1 Peter 1:8 NKJV).

1

How Do You Know?

*Those who truly believe the Gospel can never
be lost, no matter what they do.*[1]

R.T. Kendall

If you aren't already certain that you will go to heaven when you die, then it's important for you to read this book. You may *think* you have assurance of this, but how do you *know* it? More personally, if you died today, right now, would you go to heaven?

It's Vital!

Vital is defined as being necessary to life and existence. Nothing is more vital than knowing we are going to heaven when we die. Considering that the alternative is eternal separation from God in hell, what could possibly be more important in life than being assured of our eternal destination?

To be plain, those who have exercised saving faith in Jesus Christ will experience eternity with Him forever. A Christian can no more lose his or her salvation than Jesus could remove Himself from the Trinity. That's how strong a believer's eternal security is.

Real Encouragement

One of the greatest encouragements a person could ever have is to know without a doubt he or she will live with Jesus Christ in heaven forever. A Christian never has to wonder about the possibility of going to an eternal hell. In fact, biblical Christianity is the only religion on earth that teaches believers they can know with absolute assurance that they have eternal life. In every other religion it's a guessing game because salvation (however conceived) is based upon the attainment of undefined and unattainable levels of human performance.

In contrast, as one writer has observed, everyone on earth desires eternal joy and happiness—but how can this ever be certain unless one is absolutely assured that such eternal joy is attainable in *this* life? This is the kind of salvation Jesus offers freely without cost:

> God is offering us a joy that infinitely transcends all other joys combined in the power and potential to satisfy, thrill, fill, and fulfill. He is talking about spiritual ecstasy, incomparable ecstasy, unparalleled ecstasy, and unfathomable ecstasy...We must come to grips with the fact that the Bible unashamedly appeals to our desire for pleasure and happiness. And it does so because God built into us an undeniable, unrelenting, inescapable hunger for joy and satisfaction and delight. God built us to be fascinated, to be intrigued, to be exhilarated, to be stunned...You can no more escape from your desire for eternal pleasure than you can cease to be human, nor should you try.[2]

So why try?

100 Percent or Something Less?

Some have labeled the idea of absolute assurance of heaven as being naive or simplistic. They argue that spiritual truth or reality cannot have the certainty of something like a mathematical proof. We disagree.[3] If Jesus Himself told us to rejoice because our names are written in heaven (Luke 10:20) and the apostle Peter declared we have "an inheritance which is imperishable and undefiled and will not fade away, reserved in heaven for you" (1 Peter 1:4 NASB), then how could we rejoice *unless* the guarantee is absolute?[4]

God's Power and Our Assurance

*If God is for us, who can be against us?...Who will bring
any charge against those whom God has
chosen? It is God who justifies
[declares righteous]. Who then is the
one who condemns? No one.*

ROMANS 8:31,33-34

Who is greater than God?

To emphasize a point, the Bible sometimes makes an argument from the lesser to the greater. For example, regarding salvation, consider the following line of reasoning:

> Since we have *now been* justified by his blood, *how much more* shall we be saved [future reality] from God's [eternal] wrath through him! For if, when we were God's *enemies,* we *were reconciled* to him through the death of his Son, how much more, having been reconciled, shall *we be saved* [eternally] through his life! (Romans 5:9-10).

In other words, if God did the *most* for us when we were His enemies, will He do *less* for us now that we are His own dear children, purchased by nothing less than the precious blood of Christ?

Note also that in Romans 8:28-39 the argument is both logical and particularly authoritative: "If *God* is for us, who can be against us?" (Romans 8:31). Who's bigger than God? No one. Who has more authority than God? No one. Who is superior to God, having more power? No one. "He who did not spare *his own Son*, but gave him up for us all—how will he not also, along with him, graciously give us all things?" (Romans 8:32).

In addition, in Romans 8:26 and 8:34 we see that *both* the Holy Spirit and Jesus Christ are personally interceding for believers in Christ throughout the entirety of their lives. Can the intercession of both Jesus Christ and the Holy Spirit combined ever fail under any circumstances? And would God the Father give us a glorious Christ Himself and refuse us a comparative crumb?

The apostle Paul declared that nothing will separate a believer from the love of Christ: "Who shall separate us from the love of Christ?" (Romans 8:35).

Ten All-Embracing Topics

In Romans 8:38-39, Paul said that nothing will ever separate believers from God's special love for them: "death," "life," "angels," "demons," "[anything in the] present," "[anything in the] future," "any powers," "height," "depth," and "anything else in all creation."

If death can never separate a believer from Christ's love, then when a believer dies he or she is not separated from Christ's love and will go to heaven. This idea is reinforced by the phrases "neither the present" and "nor the future." Nothing in our present or future can separate us from God's love.

What's more, even angels and demons—who are more powerful than we are—cannot separate us from Christ's love. The term "powers" includes any and all additional powers that exist anywhere now or in the future, and would include our own power. The terms "height" and "depth" indicate that nothing in heaven or hell—no person, place, or thing to the extremes of "height" and "depth"—can separate us from Christ's love. Nor can any circumstances do this, and finally, "anything else in all creation." In other words, nothing can separate believers from Christ's love.

Notice in verse 31 God *Himself* has been ruled out as ever separating us from the love of Christ. The one who is infinitely wise, powerful, and loving has taken an absolute stand with believers against all others. "If God is for us, who can be against us?" Contextually, the "if" here means "since" or as the great eighteenth-century biblical scholar and theologian John Gill put it, "Seeing that He is for us." *The thought is as profound as any on earth.* Some interpreters have spoken of the idea as transcending almost everything in the human language.[1]

This nothing includes anything that the believer would or would not do during life on earth.

Think about it: Nothing *we* do and nothing done *to* us can prevent our going to heaven forever if we believe in the biblical Jesus Christ for the forgiveness of our sins. To reemphasize a point, as R.T. Kendall plainly declared, "Those who truly believe the Gospel can never be lost, no matter what they do."[2]

The Most Powerful Verse in the Bible

Some say the single most powerful verse in the entire Bible on the eternal security of the believer is Romans 8:30. Theologians sometimes call this verse "the golden chain" or "the iron chain" because it is eternally unbreakable. We like to think of it as a five-jeweled and overwhelmingly precious spiritual gold necklace worn around the neck of every Christian. There, we read that those whom God foreknew He also predestined, and those whom

> he predestined, he also called; those he called, he also justified; those he justified, he also glorified.

As can be seen from the English translation, the original Greek text of the New Testament has the words "predestined," "called," "justified," and "glorified" all in the *past* tense. As far as God is concerned these things have *already* happened.

In God's mind, every believer is already glorified. If you are foreknown (verse 28—as we will see later, this primarily means "eternally foreloved"), then you are also predestined, called, justified, and glorified.

Already in Heaven?

In other words, the believer is *already* in heaven with Christ *in this life*. In God's mind the believer is, right now, spiritually, already in heaven "in Christ." That's why noted Bible expositor John MacArthur has said, "Spiritually, the Christian becomes *a part of heaven* with full rights to citizenship *here and now in this life*," and "Because of our spiritual union with Him, we have *already entered into the heavenly realm*. We already possess eternal life, and the spiritual riches of heaven are ours in Jesus Christ."[3]

A great deal more could be said about this. But for now we should simply try and let it sink in. God says that as far as He is concerned, those with saving faith in Jesus are already in heaven with Him forever.

Do you believe it?

Assurance That Is 100 Percent or Nothing?

*We desire each one of you to show the same earnestness
to have the full assurance of hope until the end.*

HEBREWS 6:11 (ESV)

The Bible verse cited above refers to God's desire that every believer have "full assurance" of their gospel hope. When Scripture uses the term "hope," the word does not express some level of doubt as in "I hope I aced the test" or "I hope I make the team." Biblical hope is that which has been assured, that which is certain and expected but has not yet been fully realized. "For in this hope [in context, our future full adoption as children and the redemption of our bodies] we were saved. But hope that is seen is no hope at all. Who hopes for what they already have?" (Romans 8:24).

The term translated "full assurance" is also translated as "full conviction," "confidence," "full carry through," "entire confidence." As Bible commentator Albert Barnes said regarding Colossians 2:2, this word "means firm persuasion, settled conviction. It occurs only here and in 1 Thessalonians 1:5, Hebrews 6:11, Hebrews 10:22, and is rendered by assurance, or full assurance, in every instance…It was the desire of the apostle that they [Christian believers] might have entire conviction of the truth of the Christian doctrines."[1] John Wesley described it as constituting the "fullest and clearest understanding and knowledge of the gospel."[2]

By Grace or Works—Full Security or Slippery Slope?

The bottom line is that if our personal assurance of entering heaven when we die is already accomplished by God's *grace* alone, through faith alone, in Christ alone, then we can be 100 percent certain it will happen. But if our eternal salvation and assurance of heaven are achieved by our good works and spiritual performance, then we cannot be certain at all. In fact, it's impossible to have genuine assurance of our salvation based solely upon our spiritual merit.[3]

R.T. Kendall observed, "Is eternal security conditional upon [our] behavior? If so, we are back to works."[4]

If our assurance is based on good works and spiritual performance, then we face a slippery slope—so slippery that once we fall, it can become difficult to get up again (Galatians 3:1-12; 5:1-5). In other words, once we trust in our spiritual works and performance to define our eternal security and assurance of heaven, we often simultaneously lose our assurance.

The Undiscoverable and Unattainable Standard

There is a problem with basing our assurance on how well we live. If our confidence that we are going to heaven when we die is based on a certain quality or quantity of good works, plus a particular level of sanctification or personal holiness, plus perseverance in the faith to the very end in our own power (as many believe), then aren't we really teaching that our assurance of salvation comes only through our spiritual goodness, works, and efforts?

Whatever happened to grace—the biblical teaching that our eternal salvation and the assurance of it are free *gifts* that are wholly *unmerited*?[5] The Bible clearly states that our salvation and everything that accompanies it are wholly of grace alone, through faith alone, in Christ alone. Salvation and assurance have nothing to do with good works or our spiritual performance.

Many Christians believe they have assurance because of what they do. But that's not assurance; it's self-deception. Just like salvation, assurance is either based on grace or works. It can't be based upon both—it has to be one or the other. As the Bible says, if our assurance of heaven comes on the basis of our works, it is no longer based upon grace: "If by grace, then it cannot be based on works; if it were, grace would no longer be grace" (Romans 11:6). Similarly, if it is *wholly* by grace, it *can't* be by works.

Getting to the Heart of the Matter

Someone once said that the main thing is to keep the main thing the main thing. What's the main thing? To understand the truth as it relates to God's free gift of salvation by grace alone and the reality and extent of our own sin and imperfection. The Bible is clear that sin infects us from birth and permeates our being and all our actions. It is like a weight upon our shoulders until we die (Psalm 58:3; Romans 7:14-25; James 3:2). We can't do anything right.

John MacArthur points out that even though our spiritual rebirth is a supernatural one, like the raising of Lazarus from the dead in John 11, we come forth from the tomb "still bound in grave clothes." He points out that all Christians have sinful influences and are "severely troubled by them all our lives." Despite being a new person "the flesh constricts and fetters us, like tightly bound grave clothes on someone just up out of the tomb. This flesh principle is at war against the principle of the new life in Christ."[6]

Almost everyone who looks honestly at the issue of assurance and their own sin and failure understands the following truth in their heart: If our assurance of heaven is dependent upon our good works, our obedience, our spiritual growth, and our perseverance in the faith to the end of our lives, then we are in big trouble.[7] What's more, we could never have assurance that we're going to heaven when we die because we would never know if we had sufficiently met the proper standards—standards that aren't even mentioned in the Bible.

In fact, everyone has *already* and forever failed the proper standard. The only standard the Bible ever identifies is absolute, 100-percent sinless, moral perfection (see Deuteronomy 18:13; Matthew 5:48; James 2:10).

As R.T. Kendall correctly observes about good works,

> If they [good works] must precede faith—or serve
> as a condition of justifying faith—every honest,

conscientious, and transparent person would have *some* doubt whether there are sufficiently good works to warrant our claiming to be justified by faith. God puts us on our honour that we will live lives of gratitude to Him. Our sanctification is a grateful response to the gospel, not a condition of salvation. Otherwise, who can ever know for sure that he or she is saved?[8]

God either promises us the assurance of heaven purely on the basis of His grace and our trust in Christ's finished work alone, or we must seek it somewhere else. The only other place we are able to seek assurance is in what we do or don't do. But please take the time to read Romans 7:14-25 carefully, or James 3:2, or Psalm 58:3, or Isaiah 64:6, and other similar passages. See if it is possible to find assurance based on what we do or don't do.

The Most Comforting Doctrine There Is

R.T. Kendall says the doctrine of personal assurance is "the most comforting doctrine there is." After all, what could be more comforting than personally *knowing* that you are going to heaven forever no matter what?

And the reason should be obvious—because it is wholly based on God's perfect character and unfailing promises. It is based on His absolute, unchanging, eternal, and infinite love for each of His children—and not in anything we do or don't do.[9] As we will see, our assurance is based entirely upon who God is and what He has done *for* us and promised us, so that nothing is required *of* us for our salvation or our assurance of going to heaven when we die.

Further, if our going to heaven is based on something we do—anything at all—then clearly it's a matter we could boast about. But God has already ruled out any opportunity for boasting so that He receives all the glory for our salvation, as is proper (Romans 3:27).

Our eternal security and the assurance of it can never be based upon what we must do. That's precisely what makes it secure.

The Greatest Irony?

The path is smooth that leadeth on to danger.

WILLIAM SHAKESPEARE (D. 1616)

Many people are convinced they are *already* going to heaven just because they're good. Though they haven't placed personal trust in Jesus Christ for the forgiveness of their sins, they really believe they will go to heaven. This is a mass deception perhaps like no other and it explains Jesus' warning in Matthew 7:21-23: "Not everyone who says to me, 'Lord, Lord,' will enter the kingdom of heaven...Many will say to me on that day, 'Lord, Lord, did we not prophesy in your name and in your name drive out demons and in your name perform many miracles?' Then I will tell them plainly, 'I never knew you. Away from me, you evildoers!'" What's noteworthy here is these people evidently professed to be Christians.

This serves as evidence that the church needs to do a better job of explaining to unbelievers what a true Christian is. In the words of Randy Alcorn of Eternal Perspective Ministries, "For every American who believes he's going to hell, there are 120 who believe they're going to heaven."[1]

According to an extensive survey by the Pew Forum, almost 80 percent of adult Americans believe they are Christians and therefore they will go to heaven when they die. Further, about 80 million Americans claim they are evangelical or "born again" Christians.[2] Yet if you were to ask these same people why they're going to heaven, many will say it's because they are basically good.

Tragically, many who think they are going to heaven aren't. Why?

They haven't accepted salvation and eternal life on God's terms, which is through faith in Christ alone, and not good works. Then there are those who make a profession of Christian faith but have never experienced the miracle of genuine spiritual rebirth (John 3:3-8). They have made a commitment to themselves alone, not to God and His Son. They have not let God be God. So how can they possibly be saved and going to heaven? They can't.

Whatever Happened to Assurance?

Here's where the irony comes in: At the same time there are many non-Christians who believe they will go to heaven, there are many genuine Christians who aren't so sure they will make it.[3] That explains why in his book on assurance the noted Christian apologist and theologian R.C. Sproul recalls that when he was in seminary, a poll was taken of both students *and* their professors as to whether or not they *knew* that they were going to heaven—shockingly, 90 percent of both students and professors *didn't* know.[4]

Things haven't improved today. If this is what we find among seminary professors and their students, we are unlikely to find more clarity among the lay people they teach. Dr. Bob Wilkin, founder of the Grace Evangelical Society, is an expert on this issue. He recently revealed that "assurance of one's eternal destiny is now viewed as a bad thing by most evangelical scholars…The idea that a person could have everlasting life that can never be lost simply by believing in Jesus seems ludicrous to most people, even most people in the church today, even most pastors and theologians today, even most Calvinist pastors and theologians today."[5]

The oddity here is striking enough it must be reemphasized— many millions of people without the slightest reason for assurance believe they are going to heaven when their default position is actually hell; yet those who have every reason to *know* they are going to heaven have little or no assurance despite biblical affirmations that their salvation is secure.[6] Irony of ironies, unbelievers who definitely *aren't* going to heaven[7] believe they *are,* whereas *true* believers in Jesus Christ—those who definitely *are* going to heaven—wonder if they actually will. The turnabout is profound.

The Greatest Need

For believers who are uncertain whether they will go to heaven, the most important issue is to learn *why* they can be assured that they really *are* going to heaven forever when they die, with zero chance of failure. And the most important issue for unbelievers who think they are Christians but aren't is to take a much harder look at what it means to be a Christian, what being spiritually reborn really involves, and to place genuine trust in Jesus Christ alone and nothing else for the forgiveness of their sins:

> Examine yourselves to see if your faith is genuine. Test yourselves. Surely you know that Jesus Christ is among you; if not, you have failed the test of genuine faith (2 Corinthians 13:5 NLT).

> It is this Good News that saves you if you continue to believe the message I told you—unless, of course, you believed something that was never true in the first place (1 Corinthians 15:2 NLT).

First and Foremost

The first thing to do is to settle once and for all what God's mind is on the personal assurance of salvation. Does God want believers to know *with certainty* that they will go to heaven when they die—or not? After all, when an all-knowing, truthful, and never-changing God speaks on a subject, the matter is settled once and for all. There is no higher authority than that which God declares is true and promises is true.

5

What God Wants Us to Know About Salvation

*Then they asked him, "What must we
do to do the works [plural]
God requires [for eternal life, verse 27]?" Jesus answered,
"The work [singular] of God is this: to
believe in the one he has sent."*

JOHN 6:28-29

Does God *Himself* want us as believers to have absolute certainty about our eternal destiny? Is it possible to be 100 percent assured we will go to heaven when we die—no matter what happens in the future? Is there anything more vital than the answer to this question?

Thankfully, this wavering about the security of our salvation is unnecessary. God's love for the believer is infinite and eternal, and He desires every one of His born-again children to personally know, without a shadow of a doubt, that we *now* have eternal life. We possess eternal life at the instant that we place our trust in Jesus Christ. Eternal life began at the moment of saving faith and continues forever throughout eternity. Think about what is meant by the phrase *eternal life*—by definition, this life lasts forever, so at what point could it ever be lost?

To drive home the point, consider the following statement by a former devout Muslim:

> As a Muslim…It was absolutely impossible for me to
> know what God [Allah] would decide for me concerning
> Paradise [heaven]. I could have no assurance concerning
> eternity…I could not find any verse in the Qur'an that
> gave me assurance of salvation.[1]

Here is a formerly devout Muslim speaking about his personal faith prior to his conversion to Christ. His words reflect the desperate reality for virtually *every* nonbiblical religion on earth (Hinduism, Buddhism, Judaism, Roman Catholicism, Confucianism, Daoism, etc.). Because every nonbiblical religion requires good works and personal merit, it makes assurance of heaven impossible for the adherents. Why? Because it is impossible in this life to know that the standards for entrance have been met because they are nowhere clearly specified. But heaven is either a free gift by faith in Jesus Christ or something we earn on the basis of our good works—it can't possibly be both.

Unfortunately, this "earning of heaven" is also what many Christians believe. They assume that in order to have a chance of entering heaven, there are many things they must successfully perform in their actions and behavior. But even then, it is impossible for them to know with absolute certainty whether they have done enough to meet the requirements. In other words, they have, in essence, accepted the common non-Christian and anti-Christian religious view of salvation relative to the assurance of heaven.

But given the nature, character, and promises of God, how can Christians hold to such a view? Are believers willing to accept that their heavenly Father can offer no more hope to His own dear children for whom Christ Himself died, can do nothing more than all the pagan gods have offered—gods who don't even exist? If God is no different from the pagan gods relative to the critical doctrine of the assurance of salvation, then the implications are serious indeed.

The Second Most Powerful Verse in the Bible

For now, here is the second most important verse on this subject in the Bible:

I write these things to you who believe in the name of the
Son of God so that you *may know* that you *have* eternal
life (1 John 5:13).

Sometimes it is argued that because the original New Testament
Greek word translated "believe" (*pisteuousin*) may be in the present
tense, it necessarily implies the only way eternal life can be secured is
through continued believing until death. But irrespective of the doctrine of perseverance, the Greek tense is simply not definitive,[2] for
example, because the present tense simultaneously teaches the present existence of eternal life in the present moment. Such a verse cannot logically be teaching eternal life is a present possession from the
point of saving faith and also that it is only secured after continued
belief to the point of death. That would violate the law of noncontra-
diction, something even God cannot do.

Settled and Absolute Knowledge

The standard reference work *Word Studies in the New Testament* by
M.R. Vincent comments on the Greek term translated "may know"
in 1 John 5:13. It means "not *perceive* [merely to be aware of, to feel],
but know with settled and absolute knowledge."[3] Another standard
work, *Wuest's Word Studies in the Greek New Testament*, agrees that
"know" is speaking "not of experiential knowledge [knowledge based
on experience], but of absolute [knowledge], beyond the peradven-
ture [possibility] of a doubt knowledge, a positive knowledge."[4] Again,
this is 100 percent knowledge. That's why Wuest renders this verse in
his New Testament translation as follows: that those who believe in
the Son of God "may know with an absolute knowledge" that they
continue to have eternal life.[5]

True, the apostle John's emphatic declaration assumes that, for
whatever reason, some Christians might *not* have such personal assurance of their eternal salvation. But if he is teaching anything, it is
that every believer *can and should* have this knowledge of assurance—
full, unconditional assurance of eternal salvation as a present-tense
possession.

That's *why* John says it so clearly. He wants us to know that we *now* have eternal life—with "settled and absolute" conviction; "*beyond* the possibility of a doubt" knowledge. The perfect verb tense indicates "a completed verbal action that occurred in the past but which produced a state of being or a result that exists in the present."[6] In other words, God tells the believer that he or she now possesses eternal life as a present owner. This truth will become increasingly apparent in the pages ahead.

Eternal Means "Eternal"

Eternal is eternal—the original New Testament Greek word translated "eternal" in 1 John 5:13 is clear on this point when it comes to topics like God and salvation.[7] As Dr. Wayne Grudem points out in his *Systematic Theology,*[8] the Greek word is the adjective *aionios,* which means "eternal, without end."

The New American Standard New Testament Greek Lexicon states the word is found 68 times in the New Testament, and in the New American Standard Bible it is translated as "eternal" 66 times, as "eternity" one time, and as "forever" one time.[9] There is simply no doubt as to its meaning when it comes to our salvation. If we look at the most commonly used Greek-English dictionaries, Arndt and Gingrich, Thayer, or others, we find the same definition, and these are widely regarded as authoritative and determinative for the meaning of the word *aionios.*[10]

In sum, in 1 John 5:13 "eternal" means just that, and as far as our salvation is concerned, it can't mean anything else.

A Question

Here is a question to ponder: Why is 1 John 5:13 even in the Bible?

Its presence tells us something. It tells us God truly does desire that believers in Christ know and rejoice in the truth that they now have, own, and possess eternal life. If you have trusted in Jesus Christ as your Savior from sin, you now have eternal life!

Would God use *that* specific word if He knew it was possible for us to lose our salvation? *Eternal* means the following: everlasting, forever, unending, ceaseless, endless, lasting forever, never-ending, timeless, without end, of infinite duration. What's more, eternal life isn't just a quantity of life, or an everlasting existence. It also refers to a quality of everlasting life—*God's* life!

The logic is inescapable: If you have *eternal* life *now*, by definition, it is *eternal* and therefore can never be lost at any point in time or eternity—otherwise you never possessed true *eternal* life to begin with. If you ever possess it for a split second, then by definition you must possess it forever.

Put another way, if you have eternal life now, in the present, then at what point in time could you lose it? You can't, and that's the point.

That's why, if you're a Christian, you can have full assurance of going to heaven when you die.

6

No Middle Ground

Truth emerges more readily from error than from confusion.

Francis Bacon (1561–1626)

When it comes to the stated truths of Scripture, we can trust them completely and know that they will never change. That includes what the Bible says about eternal life being eternal. The reasons should be obvious. First, God Himself is eternally unchanging. He said, "I the Lord do not change" (Malachi 3:6; also see James 1:17). "Jesus Christ is the same yesterday and today and forever" (Hebrews 13:8). Second, God's Word is eternally unchanging. "Forever, O Lord, Your word is settled in heaven" (Psalm 119:89). In Matthew 5:17 Jesus said, "I tell you, until heaven and earth disappear, not the smallest letter, not the least stroke of a pen, will by any means disappear from the Law until everything is accomplished."

Nothing in heaven or earth can cancel, reverse, or annul the eternal truth and authority of God's Word. The unchanging nature of God and His Word affirms the truth of eternal security and our assurance.

Only Three Options

Only one of three options is available to us on the topic of eternal security and the assurance of our salvation:

1. We can know we are eternally secure and going to heaven when we die, or

2. We can be uncertain about the security of our salvation and eternal life in heaven, or

3. We can stay confused because the Bible seems to teach both eternal security and the possibility we can lose our salvation.

The problem with the third option is that if the Bible is contradictory, then we can't possibly trust what it says. But if God's Word is true (John 17:17) and perfect (Psalm 19:7), then it cannot contain logical contradictions. Instead, the things that appear contradictory to our finite minds are actually mysteries, such as God being three persons in one divine essence (the Trinity), the fact that divine sovereignty and human freedom/responsibility are both true, or the fact that Jesus is fully God and fully man in one Person. Mysteries are exactly what we would expect from an infinite mind. They are reconciled and understood in the mind of God, but our limited minds can only understand so much. Thus, these scriptural truths are paradoxes, not contradictions, in the same way that scientists can't understand how light can be both a particle and a wave.

Are "Problem Passages" Even Possible?

Given the fact that the changeless and truthful nature of both God and His Word are established, only one logical conclusion remains. It is this: Once eternal security and the personal assurance of going to heaven when we die are clearly established biblically, then not a single verse in the rest of the Bible can possibly teach the opposite. Practically and joyously speaking, this means no true Christian can ever lose their salvation and end up going to hell.

That means every Scripture passage that has ever been cited as evidence that a Christian can lose his or her salvation has been misread or misunderstood.[1] A major reason for this is the false assumptions people bring to the Bible when they read it. Regardless, verses that seem to teach the loss of salvation only do so on the surface;

additional study resolves the issue. The same thing occurs when one learns biblical Greek—an understanding of the language and how to translate it immediately solves all kinds of problems that seem to arise in the English text.

In conclusion, every verse ever claimed as teaching the loss of salvation must refer to a different reality—whether it is a warning about a professing Christian's false faith, the loss of eternal rewards for true Christians, a warning about divine discipline, or something else. What these scriptures *cannot* teach is the actual loss of eternal salvation once eternal life is possessed from the moment of saving faith.

Who Wants the Joy?

Believe in the Lord Jesus, and you will be saved.

ACTS 16:31

Here is the whole issue in a nutshell: Christians are either saved forever by grace alone at the point of salvation, or full assurance is impossible. There is no middle ground.

Because everything we do is always imperfect and tainted by sin, perfect holiness simply is not possible. If our assurance of salvation depended on what we do, and we still succumb to sin, what kind of assurance of eternity is possible in this life?

But if our assurance depends wholly upon the nature of the salvation that God has freely provided—upon God and what He has already accomplished for us, upon God and His utterly trustworthy promises and never-changing faithfulness and infinite power—then we can know full assurance, and spend our time and energy on simply loving God in return for saving us forever, for giving us "so great a salvation" (Hebrews 2:3).

In light of all that we have received from God, it is natural, out of love, to want to give back to Him in return. And where does that love come from? "We love because He first loved us" (1 John 4:19). So let us abide in His love (see John 15:9)—both as to assurance and appreciation.[1]

We know of no other doctrine in the Bible that is more likely to encourage joy and happiness, commitment to Christ, and godly living than the doctrine of salvation, which includes eternal security and the personal knowledge of one's assurance of going to heaven.

Assurance and Joy

Have you ever noticed that the words *joy, gladness, happiness, rejoice* and similar terms are used more than a *thousand* times in the Bible? As humans we were uniquely created for a special kind of joy that comes only from God, a particular type of excitement and delight related to enjoying God and everything He has created.[2]

Clearly, God wants His people to be happy and joyous. After all, they will inherit *Him* forever. He tells us to "*always* be joyful" (1 Thessalonians 5:16 NLT); "*Always* be full of joy in the Lord. I say it again—rejoice!" (Philippians 4:4 NLT). "I *delight* greatly in the LORD; my soul *rejoices* in my God. For He has clothed me with garments of salvation and arrayed me in a robe of righteousness" (Isaiah 61:10). "*Happy* are the people whose God is the LORD" (Psalm 144:15 NKJV). This joy, delight, rejoicing, and happiness transcends even detrimental circumstances, as pointed out by the apostle Paul in 2 Corinthians 6:10, where he said he and his fellow servants in the Lord were "sorrowful, yet always rejoicing."

Perhaps it goes without saying, but one cannot be in a state of permanent rejoicing if at any point one can lose their salvation and go to hell forever. The assurance that eternal life can never be taken from us is part of what brings us true joy; the fact of exactly who God is, His infinite love demonstrated for us at the cross, and that we are beyond-belief privileged to spend eternity with Him has much to do with that.

Just imagine being in the presence of the glory of the *infinite* God, perfect in all ways, an infinitely joyous God who loves *us* infinitely and has indescribably wondrous things planned for us forever. Even if we tried, we could never exhaust imagining the pleasures, astonishments, and gifts of such a Being, precisely because they will continue forever, time without end. In part, that will be the great thing about eternity—always being loved, always being joyous, always learning and experiencing new marvels, always being happy, forever having fun in new and different ways, only the best and better everlastingly—infinite blessings and beyond.

Thus, when we talk about the assurance of salvation, we are not just talking about something in the abstract, as if it were some fine point of theology. No, we are talking about where we will actually live forever, everything we will be doing forever, and most importantly, who we will enjoy and be with forever. As the slight revision of the Westminster Shorter Catechism by John Piper tells us, "The chief end of man is to glorify God *by* enjoying Him forever."

Do We Have the Joy?

Again, this joy isn't fleeting or based on our circumstances. It's not like worldly joy, where people are happy when their circumstances are good but unhappy or miserable when their circumstances are bad. It is circumstance-independent joy. It is a joy that, no matter what is happening to us outwardly, sustains us inwardly. When we stop to consider what God has done for us and all that awaits us in the future, we cannot help but be joyful, thrilled, deliriously happy.

And the more we learn about who God is, watch Him work in our lives during painful trials, see His faithfulness, grow in faith, understand the full implications of His infinite love and sovereignty, and accept His eternal love for us and the full truth of Romans 8:28 and other promises, the more we will come to understand that our circumstances really don't matter that much. Sure, they can be miserable, painful, debilitating. But we know who God is and what He has *already accomplished* on our behalf. We know who we are and where we're going when we die. And we know that *everything* is working together for our eternal good (Romans 8:28) and God's glory.[3] These truths can't help but bring perpetual joy to us because by their very nature they can't do anything else.

8

Having Eternal Life Now

For a person who is dying only eternity counts.[1]
FRIEDRICH DÜRRENMATT

In this chapter, we will look more closely at the truth that we as Christians possess eternal life from the point of receiving saving faith.

When we speak of the present possession of eternal life, we mean that the Bible teaches it already resides within us as Christians. It is a gift God has already given to those who have exercised saving faith in Jesus Christ. We find this illustrated negatively in 1 John 3:15: "You know that no murderer has eternal life *residing* in him" (NASB). Unsaved people cannot have eternal life residing within them. Eternal life resides only in a believer in Jesus Christ, and never an unbeliever (John 3:20; 14:7; Romans 8:9).

The Greek word in 1 John 3:15 translated "residing" is *menousan*, and according to *Strong's Exhaustive Concordance*, it means "abide, continue, dwell, endure, be present, remain."[2] Eternal life abides (remains, continues, endures) with the believer in Christ because, being eternal, it can't do anything else.

God's Promises

The present and eternal possession of the gift of everlasting life is promised by Jesus on many occasions in Scripture. That alone should settle the issue. Anything God promises us, He will deliver. If God were to promise us eternal life yet failed to keep that promise, we would *all* be lost.

Thankfully, God has given us "his very great and precious promises" (2 Peter 1:4). However, these divine promises can hardly be designated as "great" and "precious" if they never come true. Further, "all of God's promises *have been fulfilled* [note the past tense] in Christ with a resounding 'Yes!'" (2 Corinthians 1:20 NLT). Indeed, because "all the LORD's promises prove true" (Psalm 18:30 NLT), it shouldn't be difficult to believe them. Besides, God assures us that He will keep every one of His promises—eternally. Think carefully on Psalm 146:6: "He made heaven and earth, the sea, and everything in them. *He keeps every promise forever*" (NLT).[3] As an eternally changeless and infinitely truthful, holy, just, loving, perfect, and righteous God, He can't do anything else *but* keep all His promises forever—otherwise He would be a liar. And we have already seen as Scripture declares, God cannot lie. For God to lie even once is an eternal impossibility; therefore, He must and *will* keep *every one* of His promises eternally.

This means that those who have been given eternal life will possess it forever. That's a promise.

The following scriptures all are cited from the lips of Jesus Himself, who, as God incarnate, will keep these promises. For purposes of brevity we are only going to mention eight scriptures selected from one Gospel. They prove the eternal security of the believer, and therefore provide us with full assurance regarding our eternal destiny.

Eight Eternal Gems

As you read these Scripture passages, take a moment to reflect on what they are saying. And remember as you read these promises that Jesus Himself tells us His words "are trustworthy and true" (Revelation 21:5). After each promise below, you can tell yourself, "This is trustworthy and true."

It Has Happened and Is Assured

1. "Whoever believes in the Son *has* eternal life" (John 3:36).
2. "My Father's will is that *everyone* who looks to the Son

and *believes* in him *shall have eternal life*, and I *will* raise them up at the last day" (John 6:40).

3. "*Very truly I tell you*, whoever hears my word and *believes* him who sent me *has eternal life* and *will not* be judged but *has* crossed over *from death to [eternal] life*" (John 5:24).

Can you trust in the absolute nature of what Jesus has promised us in these passages—that every believer (1) now has eternal life, (2) will be resurrected to personally live forever, and (3) will not be condemned because he has already crossed over from death to life? Note the past tense of the phrase "has crossed over" (Greek, *metabebēken*)—the event has already occurred. The Greek word implies we have departed from or have been removed from one realm of existence and placed into another. In his New Testament translation, New Testament Greek scholar Kenneth Wuest rendered the latter part of this verse as "...has eternal life, and into judgment he does not come, but has been permanently transferred out from the sphere of death into the life."[4]

The Double Amen

4. "*Verily, verily, I say unto you*, He that believeth on me *hath everlasting life*" (John 6:47 NLT).

In the verse above, the original Greek text that is translated "I tell you the truth" is extremely emphatic. Jesus' use of "verily, verily" or the "double amen" prefix is employed as a firm emphasis.

There is apparently no English parallel to such usage in Hebrew literature or Jewish practice, and the intent of this "double amen" is to affirm the absolute authority of what Jesus is declaring. It's like the declaration, "Thus saith the LORD." These are solemn words Jesus uses to emphasize the great importance of what He is about to say.

Among the ways this can be rendered is "I tell you the truth," "Truly, truly," "Verily, verily, "Most assuredly," "Most certainly," "Truly,

I tell all of you with certainty," "Timeless truth I speak to you," or "In most solemn truth."

We particularly like the God's Word translation of John 6:47:

> I can guarantee this truth: every believer has eternal life.

What could be clearer?

John Gill (1697–1771), in his *Exposition of the Old and New Testaments*, said of John 6:47, "This is a certain truth, and to be depended on." Indeed, God would never have worded this verse and others like it in such a certain manner if He did not wish for believers to entirely depend upon them.

The Message translates John 6:47 this way: "I'm telling you the *most solemn and sober truth now*: Whoever believes in me has real life, eternal life." And it translates 1 John 5:13, "My purpose in writing is simply this: that you who believe in God's Son will know *beyond the shadow of a doubt* that you have eternal life."

They Will Never Perish

5. "*I give them eternal life*, and *they shall never perish; no one* will snatch them out of my hand. My Father, who has *given them* to me, *is greater than all; no one* can snatch them out of my Father's hand" (John 10:28-29).

Note the words "they shall *never* perish." The original Greek text here has a double negative for emphasis—in other words, "never, ever." Kenneth Wuest translates this, "And they shall positively not perish, never."[5]

No limitations are placed on the word "never." Why? Because the infinite power of God the Father and the infinite power of God the Son are *both* holding every believer in the palms of their hands. It's impossible to imagine anything stronger or greater than infinite power. Jesus is emphatic here to make sure we don't miss this point. God's infinite power guards the eternal security of those who trust in Him.

The Holy Spirit's infinite power is involved as well because three times in Scripture we are promised that the Holy Spirit is "a deposit guaranteeing" our eternal inheritance (Ephesians 1:14; see also 2 Corinthians 1:22; 5:5). The "deposit" spoken of here is the Greek word *arrabōn*, which refers to the promised first installment or down payment guaranteeing that the rest will certainly follow. "Vincent defines it as money 'deposited by a purchaser in pledge of full payment.'"[6] In contemporary Greek usage a modern form of this word, *arrabona*, refers to the wedding ring. With the future wedding supper of the Lamb in mind, this deposit hearkens to Jesus' promise to marry us. The Holy Spirit, if you will, is our dowry.

Vine's Expository Dictionary of New Testament Words points out of *arrabōn* that "in the NT it is used only of that which is assured by God to believers; it is said of the Holy Spirit as the divine 'pledge' of all their future blessedness...particularly of their eternal inheritance."[7]

God has given us nothing less than Himself (the Holy Spirit) as a down payment for the guarantee that we will assuredly enter heaven when we die. What more could God give to demonstrate the absolute truth that the salvation He has given us will be completed and take us to heaven? We are promised that the Holy Spirit will be with us "forever" (John 14:16). How much clearer can God be?

Our Union with Christ

6. "God *has given us* [past tense] *eternal life*, and this life *is in His Son. He who has the Son has [the] life*" (1 John 5:11-12 NKJV).

This passage promises that if we have the Son, we already have eternal life.

Life can never be had apart from God, whether physically or spiritually. Note that "the gift of God is eternal life *in* Christ Jesus our Lord" (Romans 6:23). Observe that "we are *in Him* who is true by being *in his Son Jesus Christ. He is* the true God and *eternal life*" (1 John 5:20). Jesus is *our* eternal life because we are spiritually placed into Him forever at the point of saving faith. This teaching of our union with Christ is something we will discuss more fully in a future chapter.

We Will Never Die

7. "I am the resurrection and *the* [eternal] *life*. He who believes in me will live [forever], even though they die; and whoever lives and believes in me will *never* die. Do you believe this?" (John 11:25-26).

Someday, each of us will meet physical death. But Jesus promises us here that if we believe in Him, we will live forever with God ("never die"), even though we will die physically. We will live forever with Him because not only will we "never perish," as John 10:28 promised, but "will never die" spiritually—that is, be separated from God forever. Kenneth Wuest renders the original Greek text in verse 26 as follows: "everyone who lives and believes on me shall *positively* never die."[8]

Note Jesus' question: "Do you believe this?" If you do, then you believe in eternal security—that you absolutely will go to heaven when you die.

A Love So Great

8. "God so loved the world that he gave his one and only Son, that whoever believes in him *shall not perish* but *have eternal life*" (John 3:16).

Remember, Jesus' words "are trustworthy and true."

Think about what this classic Scripture passage teaches us. It's probably the best known, most widely quoted, and most widely translated verse in the Bible in all history. But how well do we really know it?

John 3:16 tells us that God's love for the world was so great, so exceptional, so profound, so fervent, and so dear, that He sacrificed His one and only Son to make our salvation from sin possible.

There is no greater or more costly gift God could have given. Christ's death on the cross propitiated—or turned away—the infinitely holy wrath God has toward sin and turned it away forever for every person who would ever trust Jesus. Christ bore the full punishment demanded for our sins so that we would never have to pay the penalty—that's the whole point of salvation. God never saves people halfway or partially. He doesn't forgive only some of our sins. What good would that do us?

All to God's Praise

All our sins are forgiven at the point of salvation. At that time we were given eternal life, and consequently, we will never perish. As those who are in Christ, we are protected by an infinite power that sustains our eternal security. And the Holy Spirit's presence in our lives is a deposit that guarantees our eternal destiny. In light of all that, how else can we respond but with the words of the psalmist: "I will praise you forever, O God, for what you have done" (Psalm 52:9 NLT)?

What's in a Gift?

If salvation were not a free gift, how else could a sinner get it? [1]

C.H. SPURGEON

Gifts are typically fun by their very nature. There is pleasure in both giving and receiving them. That's why Christmas day is so entertaining and so much fun. That's also why heaven will be like an eternal Christmas. In the creative aphorism of Nigerian musician and educator Babatunde Olatunji, "Yesterday is history. Tomorrow is a mystery. And today? Today is a gift. That's why we call it the present."

But gifts also have a dual aspect: They are free to the receiver, but cost the purchaser.

A gift is defined as "something given voluntarily without payment in return, as to show favor toward someone" and "something bestowed or acquired without any particular effort by the recipient or without its being earned." [2]

Looking at the definition of gift in various dictionaries, we find that a gift is "meant to be free"; "the transfer of something without the expectation of receiving something in return"; "something acquired without compensation"; "something given to another voluntarily, without charge" and so forth.

There are only two things a recipient can do with a gift—either receive it or reject it. Either way, that's the end of the transaction. If it is received, then the gift has been given and it is owned. Nothing is ever required or demanded on the part of the receiver to retain it. Otherwise it isn't a gift.

Romans 6:23 tells us that "the gift of God is eternal life in Christ

Jesus our Lord." In Romans 5:15-17, salvation is referred to as a free gift no less than five times. Jesus Himself referred to eternal life as His gift (John 6:27; 10:28; 17:2).

Gifts Are Never Earned

Gifts are never earned even to the slightest degree. Rather, they are freely bestowed and freely received. Consider a wealthy husband who dearly loves and cherishes his wife.

For no other reason than loving his wife so much, irrespective of anything she has done, he decides to buy her an exceptional gift—a stunning necklace. It's made of extremely rare perfect natural pearls, not the commonly bought cultured pearls, but blue and golden Australian pearls. (The odds of finding a perfect natural pearl are about one in a million.) He has the necklace gift-wrapped with a gorgeous ribbon bow and includes a beautiful card along with the gift, in which he expresses his undying love for his wife.

Now imagine you are that husband.

Imagine yourself driving home and pulling into the driveway, with your happy wife coming out to greet you and give you a hug of affection. You get out of the car and hand your wife this superlative gift, telling her, "Here's a special something I picked out just for you, honey. After you bathe the dog, scrub the toilet, change the oil, and mow the lawn, it's all yours."

That would no longer make the necklace a gift, would it?

Conspicuous Absences

In chapters 8 and 9, we looked at eight promises from Jesus that declare we presently possess eternal life. He never *once* mentioned water baptism, good works, sanctification, growth in the Christian life, growth in personal holiness, persevering in faith to the end, or anything else except believing in Him.

This explains why God emphasizes that eternal life is a *gift*—something that, by definition, one can only receive and never earn: "The wages of sin is death, but the free gift of God is eternal life through Christ Jesus our Lord" (Romans 6:23 NLT). *Thayer's Greek-English Lexicon* defines the Greek word translated as "gift" (*charis*) as "a gift of grace; a favor which one receives without any merit of his own."[3] After all, what could any of us possibly do to earn or merit eternal life? According to Romans 3:24 the believer is "justified [declared righteous] as a gift by His grace" (NASB). Ephesians 2:8 says "it is by grace" we have been saved—"it is the gift of God." Repeatedly the New Testament identifies salvation as a gift given freely by grace.

That's why it doesn't make sense to deny the believer's possession of eternal life from the moment of salvation. Biblically and logically, such a conclusion is impossible. The only question relative to our assurance is this: Will we believe what Jesus has already *promised* us as a gift and so gain the assurance and with it the blessings it brings?

10

What Is the Nature of Saving Faith?

I gave in, and admitted that God was God.

C.S. Lewis, former atheist, Oxford University scholar

Up to this point you may have noticed the frequent use of the term *saving* faith—a term we employ as an equivalent for *biblical* faith (or belief/trust) to distinguish it from *nonsaving* faith. Jesus promises us that "he who believes *has* eternal life." But what specifically does it mean to "believe"? After all, many people claim to have "faith" in or to "believe" in Jesus, yet aren't going to heaven because the nature of their belief isn't true saving faith.

Before we look more closely at the nature of true saving faith, it's important to clarify that saving faith is not the same thing as what many people call blind faith—that is, believing something simply because we need to believe it or want to believe it for whatever reason whether or not it's true. True saving faith isn't blind. It's expressed in response to the very real and objective evidence for the truth of biblical Christianity and because of the personal work of the Holy Spirit in a person's life (see Romans 8:14; 2 Corinthians 1:22; Galatians 4:6). As noted theologian John Frame points out, "The logical probability of the truth of Christianity relative to its evidence is '1' or absolute certainty."[1]

More precisely, this is what we would call biblical faith, which is described in Hebrews 11:1. Rather we refer specifically to biblical faith: "Faith is *confidence in* what we hope for and *assurance about* what we do not see" (Hebrews 11:1). Other translations render these two italicized words as conviction, evidence, or proof.

Faith and Its Object Must Be Genuine

Both faith and the object in which faith is placed can be legitimate or not. Thus, *true* faith in a *false* Christ (as in the religions of Islam, Mormonism, Jehovah's Witnesses, and others) can't save anyone, as Jesus Himself warned (Matthew 7:22-23; 24:4; John 8:24; 2 Corinthians 11:4). People can be very committed to a false Jesus, mistakenly thinking it's the real Jesus.

Similarly, a *false* faith in the *true* Jesus Christ can't save anyone either, for "even the demons believe...and shudder" (James 2:19). Biblically, it is true that there is a faith that is not saving faith as seen in Luke 8:13, 1 Corinthians 15:1-2, James 1:23,26, and 2:14-26. Titus 1:16 speaks of those who "claim to know God, but by their actions they deny him." This nonsaving faith usually refers to a solely intellectual, purely emotional, or generally cultural or familial faith that is not grounded in personal belief in and commitment to the biblical Jesus Christ.

To illustrate, many people have grown up in Christian or Catholic homes or churches of various kinds, learning the basics of Christianity but never coming to know Jesus Christ personally. Others may have had an emotional conversion at a Christian event, but again, never trusted Jesus Christ for the forgiveness of their sins. Still others may think that because they made a "decision" for Christ in some manner that they automatically became Christians even though nothing changed in their lives. As far as their lifestyle is concerned, it is as if they had done nothing. And finally there are those who believe intellectually that Jesus Christ is the Son of God, but that's as far as it goes—He has no personal relevance to their lives. Scripture observes that the demons know well and believe the truth about who Jesus is, but they detest Him and have absolutely no desire to entrust their lives to Him (Matthew 8:29; Mark 1:24).

Biblically, What Is Saving Faith?

Saving faith is simply this: It's personal faith or trust in the biblical Jesus Christ for forgiveness of sins—a full surrender and commitment to Him. Let's expand on this to be sure we understand it.

M. James Sawyer holds a master's degree in theology and a PhD in historical theology, and has taught theology for more than 20 years at Dallas Theological Seminary. In the course of researching how to define biblical faith, he examined papyri,[2] the New Testament, and additional sources. He determined, based on those sources, that biblical faith is defined as "surrender" or "submission to." The regular New Testament meaning of believing on Jesus or being baptized into Jesus or into the name of Jesus (Romans 6:3) "means to renounce self and consider oneself a lifetime servant of Jesus" and further implies a legal transfer of ownership. Biblical faith, then, is a trust-commitment that could be considered analogous to a wedding ceremony. This is especially appropriate in light of the church being the bride of Christ: "Such evidence indicates that whatever faith is, it involves commitment. The analogy could be made to the wedding ceremony which by design establishes a new and ongoing lifetime relationship."[3]

Sawyer correctly points out that it is wrong to become preoccupied with faith because it's not our faith that saves us but it is Jesus who saves us. Our faith must be in Jesus, not in the quality of our faith. The Westminster Confession correctly says of faith that "the principal acts of saving faith are accepting, receiving, and resting upon Christ alone for justification, sanctification, and eternal life…"[4]

The late Dr. S. Lewis Johnson Jr. taught the original biblical languages and systematic theology at Dallas Theological Seminary for 31 years. He pointed out that saving faith is always the same in essence, but—and this is key—different in degree, or in quantity and quality. The amount and value of faith can vary widely. Further, unless faith is actually defined, it can mean or be almost anything, such as easy believism.[5] Reflecting the classic Reformed view, Johnson wrote, "Authentic faith, given by God, includes knowledge of the gospel's great historical facts, an assent to the truthfulness of them, and a trust in Christ who accomplished them. Is not this the faith that saves?"[6]

When the Bible refers to believing or believing in the Son, it refers to believing in and trusting the biblical Jesus Christ and what

He did upon the cross at Calvary—that He died for our sins. It is a personal commitment to who He is, a personal surrender of self to Christ. We no longer trust ourselves and what we can do, or what our church and its sacraments claim they can do, but rather trust in Christ alone for our salvation. By whatever means saving faith occurs, in essence, we come to Jesus and Him alone for our salvation, trusting in Him only.

The Greek word translated "faith" is *pisteuōn*, and its overall meaning includes the following ideas: to have faith in, to rely upon, to believe in, to entrust (as in committing oneself to Jesus Christ), to have confidence or trust in, to be persuaded, or to give oneself up in faith to. Biblical faith is simply trusting in Jesus Christ and committing ourselves to Him for the forgiveness of our sins rather than trusting anything we can do with regard to our eternal destiny.

How Much Faith Is Needed?

Among the millions of people who have become Christians since the church began 2000 years ago, not one of them ever had perfect saving faith or graduated to perfect faith during their Christian life, and none ever will. Only Jesus Christ had perfect faith all of the time.

Genuine faith can begin at any level and vary in intensity throughout one's life. Most importantly, as we will see, it can grow, and grow strong. Faith is sort of like a muscle—it grows strong with usage, but atrophies when it's not used. Further, every believer has been given "a measure of faith" (Romans 12:3 NKJV), which can then grow. But the important point is that biblically, saving faith is never perfect, meaning that our initial faith in Christ—or trust, surrender, submission, commitment—whatever word one uses, is never perfect, nor can it be.

At the point of saving faith, our actual commitment to Christ may be small indeed simply because we know so little and are such imperfect people spiritually, morally, and in every other way. Regardless, even the smallest amount of genuine faith or trust or commitment is fully sufficient to save us.

No Perfection Required

When it comes to salvation, God does not require we clean ourselves up, let alone attain an impossible moral or spiritual standard of perfection before we come to Him in faith. We come to Him as we are, and He graciously receives us.

Even the vilest sinner in the world can come to Jesus with the smallest amount of saving faith and freely inherit eternal life and everything that comes with it. The only thing God requires is a heart that sincerely seeks Him (Proverbs 8:17; Jeremiah 29:13).

At the point of salvation, it's not the words we speak to God that matter as much as the expression of our heart and that we are doing the best we can with the knowledge we have. After all, how do people who are secularists, humanists, atheists, Muslims, Hindus, skeptics, and agnostics come to Jesus Christ in the first place? How does anyone? They hear the gospel, and they respond. They inherit eternal life by believing in Jesus for salvation to the extent they are able, despite their biblical ignorance. And God accepts their sincere faith of whatever quality or quantity and they are spiritually reborn, instantly inheriting eternal life.

The Genuineness, Not the Amount or Quality of Faith

This point is so important that it demands emphasis: Biblical faith does not need to be great or perfect if the One it is placed in is already infinitely great and perfect. It's not our faith per se that saves us, it's Jesus Christ. Indeed, the smallest amount of true faith can be saving faith if it is trusting in Jesus, who is mighty to save (Zephaniah 3:17).

If figuratively speaking faith the size of a mustard seed can move a mountain (Matthew 17:20), then even a small amount of faith is sufficient to save. Again, faith can be weak but still save forever. The amount and quality of one's faith is not at issue—only the genuineness. Here's why it's so important: If we had to have a specific amount of faith or a given quality of faith, how could anyone ever know they had really been saved? If the amount of trust or commitment had to be at a certain level, it's not just our personal knowledge of assurance that is impossible, it's also our personal assurance of salvation itself. In all its 8000 verses, the New Testament never once defines or hints at some specific amount of faith-trust or commitment-surrender required for salvation.

That's why, in the Gospels, we see Jesus accepting and acting upon varying types and degrees of genuine faith. There was the thief on the cross who expressed his faith by saying only, "Jesus, remember me when you come into your kingdom" (Luke 23:42), and he was saved at that moment. There was the blind man who simply told Jesus "Lord, I want to see" (Luke 18:41).

There was the father with a son who had been severely demon possessed since childhood who, with tears and expressing doubts about his faith, declared, "I do believe; help me overcome my unbelief!" (Mark 9:24). Clearly, this man had some level of unbelief, as, in truth, we all do not only at the moment of salvation, but also throughout our lives. No one ever trusts God perfectly. That's why the apostle Paul speaks of the one who is "weak in faith" (Romans 14:1-2; 15:1; 1 Corinthians 3:1-3; 8:7-12; 9:22). Jesus also referred to the weak in faith (Matthew 6:30; 8:26; 14:31; 16:8; 17:20).

One would assume Jesus' own 12 disciples had great faith—after all, they walked with the incarnate God Himself for three years and saw everything He said and did, including all His miracles. But even they, near the end of their time with Him, still asked Him, "Increase our faith!" (Luke 17:5).

On the other hand, there was the centurion who told Jesus: "Just say the word, and my servant will be healed"—trust at which even Jesus marveled because this Gentile military commander had more faith than he had seen in all Israel. Similarly, there was the faith of the paralytic and those who brought him to Jesus for healing—faith so great they went so far as to tear up a roof so they could bring their paralytic friend in front of Jesus (Matthew 8:8; 9:2). There was the woman who had been sick for 12 years who expressed great faith and pushed her way through a large crowd and, knowing that to touch Jesus would make Him ritually unclean, desired only to touch His cloak, thinking to herself, "If I only touch his cloak, I will be healed" (Matthew 9:21).

Growing Our Faith

Faith, however weak, is something that can grow. Biblically, when faith starts out small and weak, which is common, it needs to grow in strength. Just like exercising weak muscles increases their strength, using your faith strengthens it. Abraham the patriarch "was strengthened in his faith" (Romans 4:20), and the apostle Paul commended the Christians in Thessalonica because their faith was "growing more and more" (2 Thessalonians 1:3).

Growing in our faith as a new or uninstructed Christian is something like meeting someone for the first time. We know little about this person—or in this case, Jesus Christ. What happens as we get to know our Lord better and better? As we learn more about His perfect wisdom, His nature and character, His integrity, His power, and His promises, we will come to trust Him more—and that, in turn, increases our faith. In this way we learn to "not trust in ourselves but in God" (2 Corinthians 1:9 NKJV).

The primary ways we can grow in our faith are by reading, meditating, and studying God's Word consistently; by praying daily to God (talking to Him about everything and praying for others); and by fellowshipping regularly with other Christians.

Christ Does It All

Again, our faith itself has no inherent power to save us. Faith per se never saves us—rather, it is simply the instrument of salvation. Jesus is the one who paid for our salvation. We might say it this way: We are saved by God's love and grace alone (the origin in eternity), through faith alone (the instrument in time), in Christ alone (the procurer at Calvary). Jesus is the purchaser of salvation through His atoning death, the One who actually saves us (Acts 4:12; Ephesians 2:8-9; 2 Timothy 1:10; 1 John 4:10). As Hebrews 12:2 says, Jesus is "the author and finisher of our faith" (Hebrews 12:2).[7] As the famous preacher Charles Haddon Spurgeon once observed, "It is not thy hold on Christ that saves thee; it is Christ. It is not thy joy in Christ that saves thee; it is Christ. It is not even thy faith in Christ, though that be the instrument; it is Christ's blood and merit."[8]

11

What Is the Nature of Eternal Life?

For a small reward, a man will hurry away on a long journey;
while for eternal life, many will hardly take a single step.

Thomas à Kempis (c. 1380–1471)

All life is derived from and sustained by God's eternally self-existent life. In the New Testament, the term "life" (Greek, *zōēn*) has many uses, but relative to eternal life and assurance, it refers to not just the eternal *duration* of the life, but particularly and especially to the incredibly excellent *quality* of the life.

Eternal Life Is Not Merely Eternal Existence

That this life refers to a glorious quality of eternal existence and not mere eternal existence itself is evident by the fact that Jesus apparently taught that only relatively few people would ever receive this special kind of life (Matthew 7:14). Thus, "in the books and letters written by the Apostle John and translated by the English word '*life*,' *zōē* is used almost exclusively as meaning eternal, spiritual life. An example is 1 John 5:11, 'And this is the testimony; that God has given us *eternal life*, and this *life [zōē]* is in His Son.'"[1] To repeat, this isn't just eternal existence, for even those who go to hell will have that. We are referring here to divine life. *The Bible Knowledge Commentary* accurately points out that "eternal life is a new quality of life, which a believer has now as a present possession and will possess forever."[2]

God's Own Life

There's more to this: When it comes to the gift of eternal life, God gives us part of *His* very own *life*. We don't feel it, but that doesn't mean it's not absolutely real. Whether we feel it or not, God's life is within us, both now and forever. As Bible commentator and pastor John MacArthur explains, "If you are Christian, the life of God dwells in your soul, and with it all that you need for heaven. The principle of eternal life is already in you, meaning you have title to heaven as a present possession. You have already passed from death to life (John 5:24). You are a new person."[3]

So even though we remain finite creatures forever, we also uniquely partake of God's life forever. That is the essence of biblical salvation, and that's why it is eternal from the moment of salvation. As MacArthur points out, from the moment of salvation "we have the life of God in us."[4] *Thayer's Greek Lexicon* refers to it as "of the absolute fullness of life, both essential and ethical, which belongs to God."[5] The *American Tract Society Bible Dictionary* says that Jesus makes us partakers "forever of His own life."[6]

This is why the apostle Peter tells every believer that they have "*become* partakers of the divine nature" (2 Peter 1:3-4 NASB). We, mysteriously, are inherently and eternally united with and to Christ in a way similar to water in a sponge or sap in the vine, yet much more.[7]

Both Present and Future

This eternal life is also both present and future—that is, a present possession and a future fruition. We possess it now from the point of salvation, but its ultimate expression will become far more than what we now possess. The eternal life we now possess is truly eternal, but it is only a very small part of what this life will eventually give birth to in the resurrection of our bodies and throughout eternity.

To offer a rather dim earthly illustration, this is analogous to a small seed that grows into what is considered the world's largest living tree overall, General Sherman, a giant sequoia in Sequoia National Park in California. It stands at 275 feet tall and is estimated to weigh 2100 tons.

We now possess eternal life, but it will blossom into something so loving, so sublime, so joyous, and so beautiful that it is far beyond our highest ability to imagine. We are told we will actually be like Jesus (1 John 3:2), and we will "shine like the sun" (Matthew 13:43). Miraculously and astonishingly, the Lord "will transform our lowly bodies so that they will be like his glorious body" (Philippians 3:21).

12

Going for It

*Assurance is...the birthright and privilege
of every true believer in Christ.*[1]

JOHN MACARTHUR

So far we have seen that we who are Christians already have eternal life, which is a free gift. And in light of all that this gift offers us, it is scarcely surprising for the apostle Paul to make the following exhortation: "*Take hold* of the eternal life to which you were called" (1 Timothy 6:12).

In other words, not every believer accepts the fact that they now possess eternal life or that it can never be lost. The apostle Paul, like the apostle John in 1 John 5:13, wants every believer to own and enjoy the wonderful knowledge of that reality.

We are commanded to "take hold of" (Greek, *epilabou*) eternal life. The Greek term means we are to hold it tighter, to strive to hold tightly to it, to show personal initiative and seize it, or to keep holding on, or to get a better grip on it. In other words, to really "go for it"—to take everything God has so graciously given us and run with it. In 1 Timothy 6:19 Paul repeats this thought, encouraging us to "take hold of the life that is truly life." In other words, we are to do everything we can in this life that will contribute to our eternal welfare. That's what Jesus called us to do when He urged us to lay up treasures in heaven (Matthew 6:20) that we might enjoy for all eternity. While it is not possible to lose our eternal salvation, as we mentioned earlier, it is possible for us to lose eternal rewards (1 Corinthians 3:12-15), and the apostle wants us to gain a full reward. As 2 John 1:8 says, "Watch out that you do not lose what we have worked so hard to achieve. Be diligent so that you receive your full reward" (NLT).

Consider another point. The apostle's command to hold tightly to eternal life is impossible to obey if we never had eternal life to begin with, or if there is no assurance of it or if we don't receive eternal life until after we die. No one can hold more tightly to or keep embracing what they don't already possess. So again, this is affirmation that we who are believers possess eternal life here and now.

This phrase "take hold" happens to be an allusion to the ancient Greek athletic competitions, and Paul's point, brought into the present time, means for us to hold on to the prize of eternal life as eagerly as Olympians today hold on to their gold medals—medals that were secured at enormous personal cost and sacrifice.

We should note as well the stark contrast being made here: The finite, temporal, fading prizes won by the very best athletes require literally tens of thousands of hours of grueling, merciless workouts. I (Weldon) know something of what these are like, for I used to swim competitively on the best college swim team in the nation (San Diego State University). Cumulatively, in the course of training and competition, I probably swam the equivalent of the distance from California to Hawaii. In contrast, our infinite, eternal, and ever more glorious prize as Christians (salvation) is an absolutely free gift requiring not an ounce of expenditure. (Although after we receive it, it may indeed cost us much in terms of our spiritual growth.)

But again, Olympic athletes can only hold on to something they already possess—something now in their custody. They could not hold on to something they might never receive. The only way the apostle Paul could tell us to hold more tightly to eternal life is if it's something we *already* possess as our own. As Wuest's *Word Studies in the Greek New Testament* explains:

> Now, when Paul exhorts Timothy to lay hold of eternal life, he does not imply that he does not possess it. Timothy was saved, and possessed eternal life as a gift of God.

What Paul was desirous of was that Timothy experience more of what this eternal life is in his life. The definite article appears before "life," marking it out as a particular life which the Scriptures say God gives the believer.[2]

A Simple Choice

Looking at our discussion so far, we are faced with a simple choice—we either believe what Scripture says about our eternal security—what God Himself has declared is true—or we don't, or perhaps we wrestle with it. For the sake of our spiritual peace, our growing relationship with Jesus, our spiritual fruit, our growth in holiness, and our perpetual joy, may we, by God's grace, believe what He has plainly affirmed and emphasized.

As we have noted, eternal security and the assurance that we possess it are two different things. Every believer already has eternal security from the point of salvation—whether or not they know it, even if they don't believe it. However, in order to have the personal assurance of eternal salvation, we have to believe in the promises found in the Bible—what God guarantees us. In the same way we trust in Jesus for salvation, we have to trust what God says about our assurance is true.

If we can trust God for the forgiveness of our sins and our salvation through Jesus, why can't we also trust Him for the present possession of eternal life through Jesus Christ and therefore the continuous presence of eternal life and the personal assurance of going to heaven forever when we die? The assurance of heaven *comes* through trusting God's promises.

If we believe the promises, we get the assurance—it's as simple as that.

13

Ten More Eternal Blessings

*From his abundance we have all received
one gracious blessing after another.*

JOHN 1:16 (NLT)

U p till now in our discussion about the assurance of our eternal destiny, we have concentrated on the believer's present possession of eternal life. But for additional encouragement regarding assurance, it's worth noting that the Bible tells every believer in Christ that they now possess, in the present—from the point of salvation—many *additional* blessings that are eternal in nature. As you read about these blessings, keep in mind the meaning of that word *eternal.*

Rather than explain each of these blessings, we are simply going to mention them and supply you with the Scripture references. Our hope is that you will look up each one—perhaps during your devotion time in God's Word. As you do, note that these are all eternal possessions given to us at the moment of saving faith.

1. The Holy Spirit will be with us *forever* (John 14:16).

2. We have *eternal* redemption (Hebrews 9:12).

3. We have *eternal* salvation (Hebrews 5:9).

4. We have a promised *eternal* inheritance (Hebrews 9:15).

5. We have an *eternally* interceding High Priest, Jesus, who saves *forever* (Hebrew 7:25).

6. We have *eternal* comfort (2 Thessalonians 2:16).

7. We have *eternal* justification (Romans 8:30—that is, we

have *already* been declared eternally righteous; more on this in an upcoming chapter).

8. We are called to (and will receive) *eternal* glory (1 Peter 5:10).

9. God's faithfulness is eternal and endures *forever* (Psalm 100:5).

10. God's love is eternal and endures *forever* (Romans 8:28-39).

All this is given to us because of God's abounding grace. It is as impossible to exhaust God's grace as it is His love. His grace is like an ocean, and all too often we stand at the shore with a thimble full of it when there is so much more of it available. Let us drink the whole ocean.

As to the assurance of salvation, God's electing love (Romans 8:33; Ephesians 1:4-5,11; Colossians 3:12) is particularly germane for His children's guarantee of heaven. Although we do not have the space to discuss this wonderful doctrine in here, we strongly encourage you to learn of it as well—and of God's absolute sovereignty too. Given God's infinite power, holiness, knowledge, wisdom, and love, there are probably no other biblical doctrines that are more comforting to the believer. (A good place to begin is Dr. Sam Storms' *Chosen for Life* [Wheaton, IL: Crossway, 2007]; try http://bible.org/ for some primers on sovereignty.) Indeed, it is because of our election to life that believers can know the unconditional truth of what the apostle Paul declares: "How much more will those who receive God's abundant provision of grace and of the gift of righteousness [eternally[1]] reign in life through...Jesus Christ" (Romans 5:17).

14

Astonishing

God's gifts put man's best dreams to shame.
ELIZABETH BARRETT BROWNING (1806–1861)

According to the Bible, we who are true believers have a supernatural, eternal salvation gifted to us in a moment of time. If *astonishing* isn't the right word in response to this truth, what would be the adequate term?

There is no greater gift that we could ever receive.

Four Supernatural Miracles

Christianity is a supernatural religion from start to finish and so is Christian salvation, as we will illustrate in the next four chapters.

At the point of salvation, much more than the gift of eternal life is given to believers—things totally unbeknownst to us, unless we understand the Bible.

This includes four divine miracles that have nothing to do with anything in us or anything we have done. They happen *to* us, and they happen to us even as we are evil, wicked sinners. (As Romans 4:5 says, "To the one who does not work [for salvation] but trusts God who justifies *the ungodly*, his faith is credited as righteousness.")

These four supernatural miracles share five wonderful features. They are:

1. instantaneous
2. irreversible

3. unchanging

4. indestructible

5. eternal

These astonishing supernatural events occur at the very moment of salvation. They are remarkable, freely, and graciously bestowed gifts from God that we receive at the point of placing our faith in Jesus Christ. "Every good and perfect gift is from above, coming down from the Father of the heavenly lights, who does not change like *shifting shadows*" (James 1:17).

These four precious divine gifts are:

1. regeneration (spiritual rebirth), which includes eternal life

2. eternal spiritual union with Jesus Christ

3. eternal adoption into God's family

4. eternal justification, or being made righteous forever

Each of these four miracles has an "already accomplished" and "to be expanded" aspect to them. We who are believers have already been given eternal life as a free gift; we are already in eternal union with Jesus Christ; we have already been adopted into God's eternal family as His dearly beloved children; and we have already been justified or declared perfectly righteous.

In addition, every believer is going to heaven, where each of these four gifts will be much more fully realized and personally experienced. This is why Scripture speaks of them in the past tense and also as certain future hopes or assured expectations. Because these miracles come from God in eternity past but extend into eternity future, they should astound us. It's like thinking about God never having a beginning—eventually the mind staggers at the thought as if it were intoxicated and can't think anymore.

Based Upon the Atonement

Each one of these precious miracles is true for us because of what Christ accomplished when He died on the cross for our sins—and only because of this.

Christ died for every sin we would ever commit—no matter how wicked, monstrous, or heinous—all sins past, present, and future. He "forgave us *all* our sins" (Colossians 2:13). As R.T. Kendall points out, the Hebrew word translated "iniquity" in Isaiah 53:6, "The LORD has laid on him [Jesus] the iniquity of us all," has powerful connotations—it is "a Hebrew word that covers the worst possible sin."[1] The word is *avon*, from *avah*, which means perversity, or to intentionally do wickedly. We are forgiven the worst possible sin, the worst conceivable sin.

Infinite Holiness Yet Total Forgiveness

What most people don't realize is that, given the infinite holiness of God, the penalty that perfect justice demands for even the smallest sin is eternal punishment. And in order to secure forgiveness for that one little sin, the price that perfect justice demands must be paid fully. Jesus, in His death on the cross, fully paid for all the sins ever committed by every human being who ever lived and ever will live. It is both a horrible and blessed thought—that the infinite and eternally holy Son of God would willingly take upon Himself the eternal punishment due each and every sin of billions and billions of people. Out of His immeasurable love for us, Jesus assumed the full penalty of every single sin ever committed. As Scripture says, "Though we are overwhelmed by our sins, you forgive them *all*" (Psalm 65:3 NLT).

"It Is Finished"

Jesus' last words on the cross were "It is finished" (Greek, *tetelestai*). For us, *tetelestai* is probably the most important word in all human history. It can also be translated "paid in full" and in New Testament times, this word was often written or abbreviated on the top of a bill or invoice that had been paid in full. It comes from the Greek root *teleo*, which means to bring to an end, to complete, to perfect, to accomplish to the full, to close, to finish, paid in full.[2] Christ not only fully paid the price that God's infinite holiness demanded against sin, He completely finished securing our eternal redemption. The Greek perfect tense also carries with it the idea that this fully completed past action has consequences that endure on and on, permanently, forever. As Hebrews 9:12 says, "He [made atonement] *once for all* by his own blood, thus obtaining *eternal redemption.*"

When Jesus said "Tetelestai" from Calvary, He was declaring our sin debt paid in full and our redemption finished and completed forever. It's worth noting here that the Bible never makes a distinction between the forgiveness of *past* sins, *present* sins, and *future* sins. It simply declares that if we have trusted in Christ for the forgiveness of our sins, *all* our sins have been forgiven—forever.

Future Sins

Clearly, every one of our sins was future when Christ died on the cross 2000 years ago. When Jesus died, all our sins were still future; so this must also mean that when He died, all our future sins were fully paid for. This tells us that *all* our sins are forgiven—past, present, and future, no matter how many there are. Christ's sacrifice was sufficient to cover them all. Being that He offered an infinite propitiation, His death has the power to forgive endless numbers of sins.

So no matter many sins we have committed or will commit, and no matter how bad they were or are, they have all been paid for and forgiven by Jesus, once for all. (Give Him praise and glory!)

In the words of the eminent theologian Jonathan Edwards, "God is abundantly compensated, he desires no more; Christ's righteousness is of infinite worthiness and merit."[3] As he points out, the fact that God rose Jesus from the dead and set Him at His right hand is proof enough, proof beyond measure, that Christ's sacrifice for all the sins of every believer was once and for all fully and finally accepted.

Jesus paid the full amount that infinite justice and holiness required—nothing more exists to be paid, nor can anything else ever be required of the believer because the full price has already been delivered.

May we truly accept the fact that *all* our sins are 100 percent forgiven (Colossians 2:13). As the NIV Study Bible note on Isaiah 38:17 puts it, "God not only puts our sins out of sight; he also puts them out of reach (Ps 103:12; Mic 7:19), out of mind (Jer 31:34) and out of existence (Isa 43:25; 44:22; Ps 51:1,9; Jer 50:20; Ac 3:19)." Robert N. Wilkin points out, paraphrasing John Calvin's teaching, that "Christ's death, once appropriated [by faith] finally and completely atoned for all the sins one would or ever could commit."[4]

A Loving Warning

But the teaching of absolute forgiveness of sin can never be used to take our sin lightly; God always knows what we're doing, and we can never hide anything from Him (Psalm 139:7-10). Besides, given His infinite love for us, His showering of eternal gifts upon us, and the sacrifice of Calvary and its cost, who in their right mind would ever want to take advantage of or abuse such amazing grace and love?

In addition, we must never forget that sin always has consequences in our lives. King David's life is one such example. His adultery with Bathsheba and his attempt to cover it up through the murder of her husband Uriah can logically be traced to its end in a civil war and the splitting of Israel into the northern and southern kingdoms. This is why God says, "Do not be deceived: God cannot be mocked. A man reaps what he sows" (Galatians 6:7).

Yes, it is a most precious truth that our sins are forgiven forever, and that God relates to us on the basis of grace and He clearly does not treat us as our sins deserve. But make no mistake; He will discipline His children—of that we can be sure (Hebrews 12:4-12), and His discipline can be severe. As R.T. Kendall observes, "It is a wonderful thing to know that we can never be lost; that God loves His adopted sons as much as He loves Jesus. But God doesn't like it one bit when we take advantage of this teaching. Those who abuse their rights as adopted sons can lose their reward and experience severe chastening. We must take every care that this does not happen to us."[5]

Because sin always has consequences, it's always better not to sin. But when we do sin, we must always remember our sin is eternally forgiven and, based on the results of confessing our sins to God as stated in 1 John 1:9, God has cleansed us from *all* unrighteousness and we are to move on, forgetting what lies behind (see Philippians 3:13). The Christian should *always* be free from guilt because there is always "no condemnation for those who are in Christ Jesus" (Romans 8:1).

Four Miracles Christ Made Possible for Us

Going back to what we said at the beginning of this chapter: It is Christ's death on the cross paying for all our sins (and His physical resurrection from the dead) that made possible each of the four miracles below:

1. regeneration (spiritual rebirth), which includes eternal life

2. eternal spiritual union with Jesus Christ

3. eternal adoption into God's family

4. eternal justification, or being made righteous forever

Once the sin issue in our lives was eternally resolved through our faith in Christ's death for us, God became free to give us these four gifts. We'll look more closely at each of these supernatural blessings in the next four chapters.

> *When you grant a blessing, O Lord, it is an eternal blessing* (1 Chronicles 17:27).

The Miracle of the New Birth

God just doesn't throw a life preserver to a drowning person.
He goes to the bottom of the sea, and pulls a corpse from
the bottom of the sea, takes him up on the bank, breathes
into him the breath of life and makes him alive.[1]

R.C. SPROUL

The new birth—the moment at which a person becomes a Christian, or a child of God—is a supernatural miracle. At the moment of salvation, God the Holy Spirit makes us alive to God and gives us a new nature and eternal life. This event is instantaneous, irreversible, and lasts forever. This is a work of the Holy Spirit, which is why it is said of Christians that they are "born of the Spirit" (John 3:8).

Regeneration: Raising the Dead

In John 3:3, Jesus said, "No one can see the kingdom of God unless they are born again." No one can go to heaven without this rebirth. A supernatural miracle is vital. This "rebirth and renewal" (Titus 3:5) involves taking a spiritually dead person and making him "a new creature" in Christ (2 Corinthians 5:17). As Romans 6:13 says, we *have been* brought from death to life."

Spiritual rebirth is a free gift of God that comes entirely from Him. It is a supernatural miracle because it is entirely the work of God the Holy Spirit (John 3:3-8). We are totally incapable of making ourselves alive spiritually; we can no more change our sinful and wicked nature than a leopard can change its spots (Jeremiah 13:23). We can no more impart eternal life to ourselves than we can speak the universe into existence out of nothing. Only God can raise the dead, and only God can grant eternal life.

Radically and Eternally Changed

The classic verse affirming this truth is 2 Corinthians 5:17: "If anyone is in Christ, the new creation has come. The old has gone, the new is here!" A spiritually reborn person is someone who has become genuinely new; the old person is gone. The New Living Translation renders it "anyone who belongs to Christ has become a new person."

Ephesians 2:1-10 goes into greater depth and begins by says, "You were dead in your transgressions and sins...we were by nature deserving of wrath. But because of his great love for us, God, who is rich in mercy, made us alive with Christ even when we were dead in transgressions—it is by grace you have been saved" (verses 1,3-5).

Whether we call it being born again, born from above, made alive spiritually, spiritual regeneration, a new creation, spiritual rebirth, spiritual recreation, or something similar, everything about it suggests a dramatic and permanent change, whether or not we notice it. Feelings may accompany spiritual rebirth, but they have nothing to do with its occurrence.

The very idea of this being a *birth* points toward that which is both permanent and irreversible. Once the baby is out of the womb, it can't be put back in. Just so, once we are spiritually reborn, we can never revert back to our previous condition of spiritual death because the new birth is permanent and eternal—we now have new spiritual life, the life of God, which, as we saw from our eight verses from the Gospel of John, is eternal (John 3:36; see chapters 8 of this book).

In Titus 3:5 we read that "he saved us, not because of righteous things we had done, but because of his mercy. He saved us through the washing of rebirth and renewal by the Holy Spirit." According to *Thayer's Greek Lexicon*, the word translated "renewal" (Greek, *anakainósis*) refers to "a renovation, a complete change for the better."[2]

An important point relating to the new birth is that the Greek word translated "new" (*kainos*) in 2 Corinthians 5:17 does not mean "new" simply as opposed to "old." It also means something *different*, which is exactly the point of this and similar verses.

Some Illustrations

A new car is still a car. It has the nature of a car, but it is objectively different from an old car in how it looks, how it runs, its capabilities, etc. A brand new computer still has the nature of a computer, but it is very different from a computer that is 10 years old. It can do things that were unattainable before. A new television still has the nature of a television, but it is different from an old set in terms of picture quality, variety of functions, and so on. In each case, these objects are "the same but different," and different in a variety of ways. Just so, a new creation in Christ is still a person, but he or she is *very* different from a non-Christian who remains spiritually dead in their sins and dead to the things of God (Ephesians 2:1; 4:18; Romans 8:7; James 4:4). Though Christians are new creatures, they are still people; they are made new but they still possess the fallen body inherited from Adam (Romans 5:12-18; 7:24).

At the point of spiritual rebirth, we who are Christians have been given God's life, eternal life. Through spiritual regeneration (being born again), we have a new nature that is alive to God's interests. The Holy Spirit has taken up permanent residence within us (John 14:16) and changes our concerns, interests, motives, habits, and worldview.

The Result of Regeneration: Spiritual Fruit

Despite the fact we still live in a fallen body, as new people in Jesus Christ, we are different from those who are still worldy and spiritually dead because it can't be otherwise (Romans 8:7). And because we as Christians have been made new people, there will at least be some objective evidence of our changed nature expressed in what we believe and how we live. Jesus said, "You did not choose me, but I chose you and appointed you that you should go and bear fruit and

that your fruit should abide" (John 15:16 ESV). Those who abide in
Him in their daily living "will produce much fruit" (John 15:5 NLT).
To illustrate, before a person becomes a Christian, he pretty much has
no interest in God, Jesus, the Bible, reading the Bible, going to Bible
school, church, godliness, devotions, prayer, evangelism, being baptized, communion—anything Christian or anything having to do
with Christianity. After being spiritually reborn, a person becomes
interested in all those things and can't get enough of them.

As R.T. Kendall correctly argues, "we are His workmanship, and
good works will inevitably *follow* faith."[3] They may not follow to the
same extent in every person, but they will follow. The only excep-
tions we can think of is (1) when a Christian dies before he has had
the opportunity to express his new life, or (2) when for whatever reason a believer is so backslidden he becomes completely fruitless or
so dishonoring to God that the sin unto death may enter the picture—i.e., divine discipline unto heaven (see John 15:5-6; Acts 5:1-5;
1 Corinthians 5:5; 11:29-31; 1 John 5:16).

True Faith Leads to Action

Two portions of the Bible that express well the nature of biblical
faith are Daniel and Hebrews chapter 11. In both cases, we see evidence that *faith* is a trust that leads to action. Daniel and his friends
were not afraid to live according to their convictions—their faith was
evident by their actions (for example, their refusal to worship a Baby-
lonian idol, and Daniel's willingness to be thrown into a den of lions
because he continued to worship the one true God). In Hebrews 11,
we are given a long list of people who exhibited great faith—and consistently, we see their faith spoken of in terms of their actions. Theologian J.I. Packer comments that "Knowing God, in other words,
involves *faith*—ascent, consent, commitment—and faith expresses
itself in prayer and obedience."[4] As the old saying goes, "Faith alone
saves, but the faith that saves is not alone." (Or put another way,
"Faith alone justifies, but not the faith that is alone.")

The Reformer Martin Luther—and many theologians today agree—stated that good works have nothing to do with the gift of justification (that is, our being declared righteous as Christ is righteous); nevertheless, true faith will produce good works and spiritual growth just as surely as the sun produces light. Given the supernatural nature of regeneration, and the eternal abiding of the Holy Spirit within us, biblical descriptions of faith such as in Hebrews 11 indicate that it's not really possible for a person to exhibit a "trustless faith" that is an "actionless faith."

Eternally Saved and Always Imperfect

The fact that we are a new creation in Christ doesn't mean we as Christians won't struggle with the sin nature, sin, or besetting sins. Until we die, we will endure spiritual warfare against the sin nature. But the fact of warfare also proves the truth of spiritual rebirth. To be sure, the failures of Abraham, the sins and deceptions of Jacob, the lusts of Samson, the idolatries of Solomon, the rebellion of Jonah, the evil committed by King David, and the lament and weeping of Jeremiah *over* sin and its consequences (and much more) live within us all, in fact and potential. Even the great and godly apostle Paul was still struggling with sin at the end of his life. He freely acknowledged this in the passage cited below, and every honest Christian can identify with Paul's frustrations when he said,

> The trouble is not with the law, for it is spiritual and good. The trouble is with me, for I am all too human, a slave to sin. I don't really understand myself, for I want to do what is right, but I don't do it. Instead, I do what I hate. But if I know that what I am doing is wrong, this shows that I agree that the law is good. So I am not the one doing wrong; it is sin living in me that does it.

> And I know that nothing good lives in me, that is, in my sinful nature. I want to do what is right, but I can't. I want to do what is good, but I don't. I don't want to do

what is wrong, but I do it anyway. But if I do what I don't want to do, I am not really the one doing wrong; it is sin living in me that does it.

I have discovered this principle of life—that when I want to do what is right, I inevitably do what is wrong. I love God's law with all my heart. But there is another power within me that is at war with my mind. This power makes me a slave to the sin that is still within me. Oh, what a miserable person I am! Who will free me from this life that is dominated by sin and death? Thank God! The answer is in Jesus Christ our Lord. So you see how it is: In my mind I really want to obey God's law, but because of my sinful nature I am a slave to sin (Romans 7:14-25 NLT).

Note here, clearly, that it was the sin *in* Paul, the sin nature, not the real Paul, the new creation, that was doing what was wrong (or doing evil, as in other Bible translations). The new Paul didn't want to do evil and hated it. But he had a problem with doing what was right "because of my sinful nature." The apostle Paul probably achieved a greater level of holiness than many of us do, but he didn't get full victory over sin until the day he died and went to be with Jesus.

The Bible repeatedly mentions the sins of believers; it presupposes believers are sinners until the day they die. That explains why, in the New Testament, we are given constant warnings against sin and the need to fight it. Consider, for example, the book of James. This book was clearly written to Jewish people who have become believers in Christ (1:1-2,19). It condemns the sins of filthiness and rampant wickedness (1:21), deception (verse 22), partiality (2:1-5), false doctrine (that dead faith saves), cursing (3:9-10), bitter jealousy and selfish ambition (3:14-16), quarrels and fights (4:1), murder and coveting (4:2; see also 2:10-12), wrong motives (4:3), friendship with the world and spiritual adultery (4:4), pride (4:7-12), arrogance (4:13-16), grumbling (5:9), and potential backsliding (5:19-20).

All Christians will continue to struggle against sin nature until the day they die; that's when the sinful nature is finally removed forever. It's impossible to become morally perfect before this time. That's why Martin Luther coined his famous phrase "simultaneously just [declared righteous] and a sinner"—or, "at the same time justified and sinful."

Unfortunately, some people in the church—such as revivalist Charles Finney and Methodist founder John Wesley—have taught the doctrine of virtual perfectionism, an unattainably high state of sanctification (cleansed from original sin, made free from inbred sin, perfected in love, entire sanctification, etc.). The Princeton theologian Benjamin B. Warfield wrote an excellent response to such teachers in his book *Perfectionism*.[5] Although the work is more than a century old it remains highly relevant. Unfortunately, those who hold to the doctrine of perfectionism may find it easy to deceive themselves either by redefining sin (if one exists in a state of extreme sanctification but is still sinning, it's easy to reclassify one's sins as less than sinful), or by rejecting sin altogether. But the Bible teaches otherwise (see 1 John 1:8-10), as does the experience of Christians for more than 2000 years. We can't read the writings of even the greatest Christians too long before discovering that they saw themselves as great sinners before God. All this explains why A. Bierce put it well when he defined death as "To stop sinning suddenly."

The esteemed theologian Jonathan Edwards observed that when it came to pleasing God he was keenly aware of his "extreme feebleness and impotence." In addition, he was frank about "the innumerable and bottomless depths of secret corruption and deceit" within his heart.[6] At the age of 82, near the end of his life, the great John Newton observed, "My memory is nearly gone, but I remember two things: that I am a great sinner—and that Christ is a great Savior!" Other highly regarded Christian leaders, such as Martin Luther, John Calvin, Richard Baxter, D.L. Moody, C.H. Spurgeon, and Billy Graham spoke in the same manner.[7]

It all goes to show that the struggles Paul wrote about in Romans 7 will remain true about us until the day we die. That's why the famous Sir Walter Raleigh, waiting in the Tower of London for his execution, wrote:

> And when the grand 12 million jury
> Of our sins, with direful fury,
> Against our souls black verdicts give,
> Christ pleads His death, and then we live.

We Will Win

In the interim before heaven, we as Christians not only live in a foreign land (1 Peter 2:11), we have three formidable enemies: the world, the flesh, and the devil. Moreover, we are told that our "enemy the devil prowls around like a roaring lion looking for someone to devour" (1 Peter 5:8). Yet God promises that He will make all things work together for our eternal good and His glory—so that no matter what happens, in the end, we will win (Romans 8:28). That's made possible because Christ has already secured for us—in His death and resurrection—the ultimate victory over all the things of the world, the flesh, and the devil.

That's a miracle!

The Miracle of Our Eternal Union with Christ

There is no legal [or other] loophole by which God is able to get out of His pledge to save those who have believed on His beloved Son. He can't, and He won't...[Believers] have taken up residency in heaven. We are "in Christ," and Christ is at the right hand of God, the Father. We cannot be thrown out of heaven unless Christ Himself were to be thrown out.[1]

ERWIN W. LUTZER

In a sense that we don't fully understand, God spiritually raises up every believer and places him or her "into Christ" from the moment of saving faith.[2] This miracle—our union with Christ—is instantaneous from the moment of saving faith. It is also irreversible and eternal. Nothing in heaven or on earth—including our own actions—can ever take us out of Christ. We are united to Him forever. This is not mere symbolism or a figure of speech; it is an actual, mysterious union.[3] Think of it this way: If each person of the Trinity mutually indwells one another, and the Holy Spirit indwells us, then Christ indwells us as well (technically, through the Holy Spirit). As 1 John 4:13 says, "By this we know that we abide in Him, and He in us, because He has given us of His Spirit" (NKJV).

This doesn't mean we are absorbed into God in such a way that we lose our personal identity or individuality, or that we are "becoming God" in the sense that many Eastern religions teach. We are never incorporated into the life of the immortal Godhead in the sense that we partake of the essence of deity. Yet at the same time, our union is more than an intellectual, positional truth.

A Foundational Teaching

Our union with Christ is an actual and vital spiritual union. In *Redemption: Accomplished and Applied*, theologian John Murray, who taught at Princeton Seminary and helped found Westminster Theological Seminary, referenced our union with Christ as nothing less than the central truth of the Christian doctrine of salvation. Theologian John Owen[4] said likewise. The believer's justification, adoption, regeneration, and more result from or presuppose our being "in Christ"—in union with Him. Owen referred to our "union with Christ [as] a spiritual conjugal bond effected by the Holy Spirit."[5] The doctrine is much more profound than can be suggested here.[6] Indeed, all the blessings we have spiritually (some of which we have discussed in this book) are because of our union with Christ. For example, consider how the New Living Translation translates Ephesians 1:3: "God…has blessed us [past tense] with *every* spiritual blessing in the heavenly realms *because* we are united with Christ."

The phrases "in Christ," "in Christ Jesus," "in Him," and similar expressions occur almost 250 times in the New Testament. Clearly, the fact this union is mentioned so frequently tells us something very important is being emphasized. Indeed, as C.S. Lewis asked, "Once a man is united to God, how could he not live forever?"[7]

A More Substantial Reality

Jonathan Edwards once remarked concerning the relationship of the Father to the Son, "Christ is a person exceedingly dear to the Father, the Father's love to the Son is really infinite. God necessarily loves the Son; God could as soon cease to be, as cease to love the Son. He is God's elect, in whom his soul delighteth; he is his beloved Son, in whom he is well pleased; he loved him before the foundation of the world, and had infinite delight in him from all eternity."

Edwards then proceeded to demonstrate the logical consequences for those who are "in" God the Father's eternally beloved Son, Jesus Christ:

> Christ is a person so dear to the Father, that those who are in Christ need not be at all jealous [concerned] of being accepted upon his account. If Christ is accepted they must of [necessary] consequence be accepted, for they are in Christ, as members, as parts, as the same. They are the body of Christ, his flesh and his bones. They that are in Christ Jesus, are one spirit [with him]; and therefore, if God loves Christ Jesus, he must of necessity accept those that are in him, and that are of him. [8]

As a result, "A terrified conscience, therefore, may have rest here, and abundant satisfaction that he is safe in Christ, and that there is not the least danger but that he shall be accepted, and that God will be at peace with him in Christ." [9]

Our union with Christ refers to the believer's spiritual position "in Christ" and involves something *more* substantial than our physical reality and being. Our physical reality, our body, will eventually return to the dust of this earth. But this is not true for our union with Christ. The spiritual reality we are talking about is infinitely durable because it is united to God Himself. If we are believers, this union (1) exists now at this present moment; (2) it can never be dissolved because, though finite as to our personal reality, it carries, so to speak, the "reality" and "weight" of God Himself; and (3) it is eternal (see endnotes 3 through 6 for this chapter).

The very reason believers can now *know* that they possess eternal life is because at the very moment of spiritual rebirth we were eternally placed into Christ and united with Him forever. This is our true home and our greatest reality—even though we sense nothing about it psychologically or physically. That's why Christ "*is* our life" (Colossians 3:4).

True Life Is Found Only in Christ

The extraordinary kind of life spoken of in the new birth is obtained only through actual union with and in Jesus Christ. We earlier saw it is God's own life. This explains why there are only two kinds of people in the world: those who are in Christ and those who are not. "This is the testimony: God has given us eternal life, and this life is *in His Son*. Whoever *has* the Son *has* life; whoever does *not* have the Son of God does *not* have life" (1 John 5:11-12).

Only God is immortal (1 Timothy 6:16), which means eternal life can be found *only in Him*. By definition, eternal life qualitatively and quantitatively can never be found in anything created or finite, but only in God. For believers, eternal life is never something granted independent of Jesus Christ or granted in the future upon death or at the resurrection. If it were, Scripture could not speak of believers as being "in Christ" now.

The reason Scripture tells us that Jesus Christ is our eternal life is because that's the only place eternal life could possibly reside—in the immortal Jesus Christ Himself. As John Calvin observed correctly, "We must not imagine that there is life anywhere [other] than in God."[10]

As 1 John 5:11 says, "This is the testimony: God has given us eternal life, and this life is in his Son" (see also John 14:6; 1 John 1:2,4).

The Safest Place in the Universe

The very reason we cannot lose our salvation by anything we do or experience, or anything the devil does, is precisely because we are in Christ—the safest place in the whole universe. If by definition and nature our union with Him, once instituted, is eternal, then that's it—we *have* eternal life, and therefore it can logically never be lost. "He who believes *has* eternal life" (John 6:47) is a truth as simple as sugar—and yet as profound as God Himself.

That is the reason we find such strong language relative to our assurance of salvation as in Romans 8:28-39 and other passages—because being eternally "in Christ" means we are forever safe from *everything* outside of Christ.

Union with Christ Necessitates the Presence of Eternal Life

From the point of eternal union with Christ, the believer can never suffer eternal separation from God. The life God has given us is described as eternal because it is life *in Christ*, the life of God Himself and a life that is never found apart from Him. Because God's life is forever and eternal, so our life is and must be forever and eternal once we are united to Christ or in Christ. Even God could not prevent us from going to heaven given this kind of spiritual reality, not to mention according to His immutable holy nature and promises.

Put another way, because believers are in Christ (actually in the Trinity itself), it would be impossible for us *not* to partake of God's own life, which involves eternal life. If we could die eternally, God could die eternally, something that's impossible. Our union with God is so powerful, so unbreakable, so binding and eternal that if as a believer we could ever go to hell in judgment, God would have to go as well. We are so united to the Trinity that we could no more be removed from it then one of the divine Persons could be removed from it.

As Kendall correctly reasons, "our security in the family as children of God is as strong as that of Jesus in the Godhead."[11] And as Erwin Lutzer observed at the beginning of this chapter, we have already taken up residency in heaven and "we cannot be thrown out of heaven unless Christ Himself were to be thrown out."

That's security.

Scriptural Proof

Here are just a few of the 250 scriptures that speak of our union with Christ:

He raised us from the dead along with Christ and seated us *with him in the heavenly realms* because *we are united with Christ Jesus* (Ephesians 2:6 NLT).

You also were *included in Christ when you heard the message of truth*, the gospel of your salvation. When you believed, you were marked in him with a seal, the promised Holy Spirit (Ephesians 1:13).

You have been *raised with Christ*... (Colossians 3:1).

You died to this life, and your *real life is hidden with Christ in God* (Colossians 3:3 NLT).

The New Testament uses various analogies and figures of speech to convey the concrete reality of our enduring union with Christ, language never used of the angels, who are never said to be in Christ. For example, Jesus taught that He is the vine and believers are the branches, signifying an organic unity: "Yes, I am the vine; you are the branches" (John 15:5 NLT).[12]

Body and Bride

Our spiritual union is why the true (invisible) church is defined as Jesus' own "body" (Romans 12:5; 1 Corinthians 12:27) and as His unique "bride" (Ephesians 5:23,27,32; Revelation 21:9). "Body" and "bride" constitute powerful imagery. The reality of our union with Christ can hardly be affirmed in more intimate language:

Do you not know that *your bodies are members of Christ* himself? (1 Corinthians 6:15; see also Ephesians 5:30).

He who is *joined to the Lord becomes one spirit with Him* (1 Corinthians 6:17 ESV).

All of you together are *Christ's body*, and *each of you* is a part of it (1 Corinthians 12:27 NLT; see also 1 Corinthians 12:12; Ephesians 1:23).

He is the *head of the body, the church* (Colossians 1:18 cf., 2:19).

God placed all things under his feet and appointed him to be head over everything for the church, *which is his body, the fullness of him* who fills everything in every way (Ephesians 1:22-23).

From the moment of salvation onward believers are members of Christ's own body. As noted earlier, the word Greek word translated "partakers" in "partakers of the divine nature" (2 Peter 1:4 NKJV), *koinōnoi*, also means and been translated as "partners," "companions," "sharerers" and "fellow-partakers." It means to be one's partner in.

The Bible teaches us that we are organically and spiritually united to Jesus Christ at the moment of saving faith. As a result, "if we are faithless, he remains faithful, for he cannot disown himself" (2 Timothy 2:13). When the apostle Paul used the phrase "cannot disown himself," he was referring to Christians, who cannot be disowned because they are members of Christ's own body.

As a church, we are individually and collectively headed toward a wedding ceremony beyond all others, as the bride of Christ at the wedding supper of the Lamb (Revelation 19:7,9)—and the reception will be a party like none ever held on earth.

> *I will betroth you* to me forever; *I will betroth you* in righteousness and justice, in love and compassion (Hosea 2:19).

> Come, I will show you *the bride, the wife of the Lamb* (Revelation 21:9).

> As a bridegroom rejoices over *his bride,* so will your God rejoice over you (Isaiah 62:5).

The image of *both* body and bride is presented in Ephesians 5:31-32: "'For this reason a man will leave his father and mother and be united to his wife, and the two will become one flesh.' This is a profound mystery—but *I am talking about Christ and the church.*"

If Christ is depicted as the head of the church, His body, then parts of His body are unlikely to become detached from Him—ever. A spiritual body can't be sliced up, nor would God ever do such a thing when His Son died for it in the first place.

Given the nature and reality of body, marriage, and physical union in marriage, for God to describe His people as Christ's body and Christ's bride and becoming "one flesh" with Him suggests nothing less than full assurance. The church, individually and collectively, is the body of God's own dear Son. Further, God says, "I hate divorce" (Malachi 2:16 NASB). Because the church is the bride of God's own dear Son, it is unthinkable that Jesus Christ would ever divorce His own bride, whom He gave His life for.

The Family of God

Husband and wife, bridegroom and bride, and head and body are not the only ways in which God powerfully describes the intimacy of the relationship between Him and the children He loves.

- There is also the father and child relationship (1 John 3:1; Ephesians 1:5)

- Jesus Christ Himself called us His own brothers and His true family (Mark 3:33-35; Romans 8:29; Hebrews 2:11)

- We are "heirs of God and co-heirs with Christ" (Romans 8:17; 2 Timothy 2:12)—we will inherit, in some sense, His very own glory (Romans 8:17; 9:23; 2 Thessalonians 2:14)

God's Temple and Building

Believers are also figuratively declared to be the temple of God—God's indwelling and building. Anyone who has studied about the Old Testament temple understands how important it was to God, that it was a replica of the temple in heaven (Hebrews 8:5; 9:23). And yet this is the imagery we find for every believer in Christ.

Consider the following verses. As amazing as it is, all believers are said to be the holy dwelling place of God Himself:

> We are the *temple* of the living God (2 Corinthians 6:16).

> Don't you know that you yourselves are God's *temple* and that God's Spirit dwells in your midst? (1 Corinthians 3:16).

> Do you not know that your bodies are *temples* of the Holy Spirit, who is in you, whom you have received from God? You are not your own…(1 Corinthians 6:19).

> In him the whole building is joined together and rises to become a holy *temple* in the Lord. And in him you too are being built together to become a dwelling in which God lives by his Spirit (Ephesians 2:21-22).

> If anyone destroys God's *temple,* God will destroy that person; for God's *temple* is sacred, and *you* together are that *temple* (1 Corinthians 3:17).

In 1 Corinthians 3:9 the church is described as God's "building." God is in the process of building His eternal temple, the one in which He will dwell forever. This temple has been in His mind from all eternity—to conceive of even one missing stone or brick is unimaginable. It is God's holy temple and (like His Son), in eternity, it will be without spot or blemish. Note the extreme precision, care, and detail given to building the Old Testament temple—merely a physical building, glorious as it was. How much more care will God assume for His eternal temple comprised not of perishable things, but of living stones, souls redeemed by the precious blood of Christ? "You also, like living stones, are being built into a spiritual house to be a holy priesthood" (1 Peter 2:5).

And there's more.

Mutual Indwelling

Jesus' prayer for all believers before His crucifixion was that they would "be one"—"just as you are in me and I am in you. May they also be in us... [and may they] be one as we are one—I in them and you in me—so that they may be brought to complete unity. Then the world will know that you sent me and have loved them even as you have loved me" (John 17:20-23).

The Bible teaches that each person of the Trinity mutually indwells one another in a holy and loving communion that has existed forever. And every believer in Christ dwells within each person of the Trinity as well. Because we are in Christ, we are simultaneously in the Father (John 14:23) and in the Holy Spirit (John 14:17; Romans 8:9).

With all that in mind, how should our union with Christ affect the way we live? The apostle Paul gives the answer in Philippians 2:1-4:

> If you have any encouragement from being united with Christ, if any comfort from his love, if any common sharing in the Spirit, if any tenderness and compassion, then make my joy complete by being like-minded, having the same love, being one in spirit and of one mind. Do nothing out of selfish ambition or vain conceit. Rather, in humility value others above yourselves, not looking to your own interests but each of you to the interests of the others.

The Miracle of Our Eternal Adoption into God's Family

Our security in the family as children of God
is as strong as that of Jesus in the Godhead.[1]

R.T. KENDALL

Divine adoption is a supernatural miracle because it is the exclusive act of God whereby He legally adopts us into His eternal family on the basis of the finished work and merits of Jesus Christ. It is instantaneous, once for all, irreversible, and lasts forever. Think of it this way: God has already signed the legal adoption papers and made us the legal heirs of everything He owns. In His mind, He has already brought us home to live with Him and is simply awaiting our actual arrival in heaven. This is why Psalm 116:15 declares, "Precious in the sight of the LORD is the death of His saints" (NKJV).

Adopted and Beloved

If adopting a child represents anything, it represents unconditional love. For a priceless orphaned baby to be adopted by a husband and wife is one thing. But for wholly undeserving and morally evil men and women to be eternally adopted by an infinitely holy God Himself into an eternal family is an entirely different order of things.

The very idea is staggering—that the infinite God would personally and permanently adopt once-rebellious people as His own children—and not in the sense of being adopted through some impersonal third-party adoption agency, but intimately and personally as His own dearly beloved children. Consider the following verses:

In Christ Jesus you are all children of God through faith (Galatians 3:26).

God decided in advance to adopt us into his own family by bringing us to himself through Jesus Christ. This is what he wanted to do, and it gave him great pleasure (Ephesians 1:5 NLT).

You have not received a spirit that makes you fearful slaves. Instead, you received God's Spirit when he adopted you as his own children. Now we call him, "Abba, Father" (Romans 8:15 NLT).

See how very much our Father loves us, for he calls us his children, and that is what we are! (1 John 3:1 NLT).

To all who did receive him, to those who believed in his name, he gave the right to become children of God (John 1:12).

Those who are led by the Spirit of God are children of God.... The Spirit himself testifies with our spirit that we are God's children (Romans 8:14,16).

An Eternal Arrangement

How do we know our adoption is eternal, something both illustrating and expressing God's eternal love for us? Because our election is eternal (Matthew 25:34; Ephesians 1:4-12; 2 Timothy 1:9), and because all the varied doctrines we have been discussing that speak of the certainty of our eternal relationship with God from the moment of salvation are interrelated and indissoluble, incapable of being severed.

We saw an example of this in Romans 8:30, where we read this about every believer: "Those he predestined, he also called; those he called, he also justified; those he justified, he also glorified." That our glorification is spoken of in the past tense means it is an absolute certainty.

If we look one verse earlier at Romans 8:29, we read that "those God foreknew he also predestined to be conformed to the image of his Son." R.C. Sproul noted that the word "foreknew" carried this significance for the believer:

> From all eternity God foreknew His elect. He had an idea of their identities in His mind before He ever created them. He not only knew them in the sense of having a prior idea of their personal identities, but He also foreknew them in the sense of foreloving them. We must remember that when the Bible speaks of "knowing" it often distinguishes between a simple mental awareness of a person and a deep intimate love of the person.[2]

Clearly, the foreknowledge spoken of in Romans 8:29-30 could not refer to simple omniscience, for God absolutely knows unbelievers just as well as He knows believers—which would mean unbelievers would automatically be glorified and saved forever based on this definition of foreknowledge. Thus the apostle Paul must be referring to a different kind of foreknowledge.

Erwin Lutzer agrees that "foreknew" in Romans 8:29 means those people whom God "set His affection on" and those He "foreloved"— those *already* intimately and deeply cherished by God in eternity past.[3] All this explains what Paul wrote in Ephesians 1:3-14 about this love being precious, eternal, and infinite (see also John 15:9; 17:23).

We can also marvel over the fact this adoption was determined by God in eternity past, before we were born. Even more astounding is what this adoption means for us in eternity future. The fullness of all that awaits us in heaven has yet to be revealed, although Scripture suggests it is beyond anything we can imagine:

> Dear friends, now we are children of God, and what we will be has not yet been made known. But we know that when Christ appears, we shall be like him, for we shall see him as he is (1 John 3:2).

The Miracle of Our Eternal Justification

Simul iustus et peccator.
("At the same time just and a sinner.")

MARTIN LUTHER (1483–1546)

The doctrine of justification is one of the most profound, joyous, and exhilarating doctrines found in the Bible. Simply stated, *justification* is a one-time legal declaration in which God declares a believer righteous based on Christ's righteousness. At the moment of saving faith, a person is declared justified. This too is instantaneous, absolute, irreversible, and lasts forever.

Justification is a supernatural miracle with results that continue and never end. It's as if you have *already* stood before God in heaven, before His tribunal, the ultimate high court, and He has officially and legally pronounced you "Not guilty" forever—all because of what Christ did on the cross.

Scriptural Proof[1]

Consider the following scriptures that declare that our justification is a past, once-for-all, completed action with results that continue forever. Justification continues eternally because God justifies us or declares us righteous as *a gift* (we are "justified by His grace as a gift"—Romans 3:24 ESV). And we already know that "the gifts and the calling of God are irrevocable" (Romans 11:29 ESV)—or, as the New Living Translation puts it, "God's gifts and his call can never be withdrawn."

> Since we *have been justified* through faith, we [always] have peace with God through our Lord Jesus Christ (Romans 5:1).

> Much more then, *having now been justified* by His blood, we *shall* be saved from the wrath of God through Him (Romans 5:9 NASB).

> You were washed, you were sanctified, *you were justified* in the name of the Lord Jesus Christ and by the Spirit of our God (1 Corinthians 6:11).

> He made Him who knew no sin to be sin on our behalf, so that we might become the righteousness of God *in Him* (2 Corinthians 5:21 NASB).

In fact, justification involves a *double* imputation or divine crediting on our behalf. First, *all* of our sins and guilt were imputed or reckoned to Christ and placed to His account, which happened on Calvary when He bore their unspeakable cost. Second, *all* His perfect righteousness and obedience are imputed or credited to our account upon saving faith.

Justification Illustrated

To illustrate, imagine that you are somehow $100,000 in debt and overdrawn $10,000 on your personal bank account. Because you live in the thirteenth century, you are headed to a debtor's prison for the rest of your life. Your spouse is apoplectic, the kids have locked themselves in the closet, and even the dog can't stop howling. You know you are in big trouble. But before the jailers arrive to take you away, an incredibly wealthy landowner contacts your banker. He wants your banker to inform the bankruptcy court that he desires to join *his* account to your account. What belongs to him now belongs to you—legally.

When his account is transferred or credited to your account, what will happen to all your debt? It will be covered by the landowner's vast riches—it will disappear forever. But having your debts forgiven isn't all that happens. What about your status? You will no longer be treated as a criminal and pauper; rather, you will be treated as a wealthy landowner as well. Because a rich man has joined his bank account to yours, you really *are* rich—even though you never earned a penny of it.[2]

In justification, God freely "deposits" the entire righteousness of Jesus Christ to the believer's account. That is, God legally imputes, credits, or transfers to the believer's spiritual standing the 100 percent perfect moral sinlessness and righteousness of His own Son—even though the believer never earned a penny of it.

An Eternal Result

R.T. Kendall accurately refers to the fact that "the righteousness of Christ is put to our credit forever."[3] Erwin Lutzer tells us that "justification means that I have been declared as righteous as Christ Himself and will be considered as such for all of eternity." He goes on to point out that we have been "declared just as righteous as God. And the [eternal] Judge has already agreed to accept the terms of the acquittal."[4]

Justification is legally applied and occurs simultaneously with saving faith. Although given at the point of regeneration, nevertheless, in the mind of God, it has existed forever for the believer—and will exist forever in the future. It is God's final judgment brought into the present and extended forever into the future. Our justification—being declared as righteous as God is righteous—isn't temporal. It is never-ending, a gift from God that we carry with us eternally.

The Difference Between Justification and Sanctification

Justification is God's declaring us righteous at the moment of salvation. In His eyes, we are as righteous as Christ. *Sanctification*, however, is our everyday growth in living out the Christian life. It includes growing in our faith and commitment to Christ, and maturing in personal holiness. Justification has to do with our standing before God, whereas sanctification is our cooperating with God and living out the Christian life in appreciation for all He has done for us.

The more we fall in love with God, the more He will mean to us personally and the more we will live for Him. In other words, the more we understand who He is in truth, the more we will trust Him in everything, including life's trials. The more we understand everything that God so lovingly and sacrificially has *already* done for us forever "in Christ," the greater our gratitude, which we express by living as God calls us to live. As R.T. Kendall observes, "The doctrine of sanctification is the doctrine of gratitude."[5] Gratitude and trust in His never-ending grace is the open door to spiritual abundance.

Biblically, every believer in Christ *has already been* (past tense) justified from the moment of saving faith. Therefore the Catholic Church is wrong when it teaches that believers are not justified until they are first personally *made* righteous by good works and individual holiness. When Pope John Paul II said that "a good life is the *condition* of salvation,"[6] he was opposing biblical teaching. Justification, biblically speaking, *never* means "to make righteous"—it always means "to declare righteous" forensically or legally, as New Testament Greek dictionaries prove.[7] And it is granted to us when we as evil and wicked people receive Christ as Savior—not after we have tried to clean up our act, something that we can never do on our own ability anyway.

The health of the church rests upon the doctrine of justification, but tragically, many Christians know little about it or seldom hear about it in their churches. R.T. Kendall has noticed this, saying, "In my travels all over the world I have been increasingly alarmed at how vague the teaching on justification by faith is in churches and how few people grasp it."[8]

Such a precious truth should never be so squandered.

Justification and Our Union in Christ

Justification is inherently connected with our union with Christ:

> God made him who had no sin to be sin for us, so that
> *in him* we might become the righteousness of God
> (2 Corinthians 5:21).

> It is because of him [God] that you are in Christ Jesus,
> who has become for us wisdom from God—that is, *our*
> *righteousness, holiness and redemption* (1 Corinthians 1:30).

As Sinclair Ferguson, a professor of systematic theology, points out, "Justification takes *place only in union with Christ*...in this union in which we *are justified*, Christ who *becomes our righteousness also becomes our holiness or sanctification* (1 Corinthians 1:30)."[9]

Referencing 1 Timothy 3:16 and Romans 4:25, Ferguson further explains,

> God's verdict on Jesus will be neither reversed nor
> repeated. It was once and for all—final. But precisely
> because we are justified in Him—that is, in His justi-
> fication—our justification is also final and irreversible.
> Indeed we can be so bold as to say that we are as *fully* jus-
> tified before God as our Lord Jesus is. We are as *finally*
> justified as our Lord Jesus is. We are as *irreversibly* justi-
> fied as our Lord Jesus. The only justification we have—
> our only righteousness—is that of the Lord Jesus. We
> are justified with His justification...Our righteousness
> is a complete and final righteousness that *encompasses all
> eternity*.[10]

This is why we read in Hebrews 10:14, "By one offering [Christ] has perfected for all time those who are sanctified [that is, who are now increasing in their spiritual growth]" (NASB).

In God's eyes, Christ's perfect righteousness has been reckoned to our account, and thus we stand before God perfectly righteous.

That is why, as Romans 8:1 says, "There is now no condemnation for those who are in Christ Jesus." The doctrine of justification is yet another reason we can have complete assurance that we are going to heaven. Nothing will change our eternal destiny; it's an issue that's settled forever.

19

Accept, Cherish, and Relish God's Love for You

*Nothing binds me to my Lord like a
strong belief in his changeless love.*

C.H. Spurgeon (1834–1892)

*L*ove is one of the most powerful words in the human language. And *true* love is what everyone yearns for more than anything else in life. Mark Twain put it this way: Love is "the irresistible desire to be irresistibly desired." However it's defined, we can pretty well agree that everyone wants to be loved and accepted—they want other people to like them. That's a truly universal human sentiment.

But for whatever reason, perhaps you have a hard time believing God really loves *you*. It may be because you grew up an orphan, or because you struggle with sin and guilt, or because you've faced very difficult circumstances. For some reason or other, you have doubts about whether God loves you.

And yet in all eternity God can never love you any more than He does now—nor can He ever love you any less. As the early church father Augustine said, "God loves each one of us as if there were only one of us to love."

What If I Don't Feel Saved?

Sometimes Christians don't feel loved, or feel saved, let alone assured of eternity in heaven. Sometimes this feeling can run deep, depending on a number of factors. Every Christian goes through this at some time or other, to some degree, even the greatest. C.H. Spurgeon's bouts with depression were legendary, as were Martin Luther's struggles with guilt. Likewise, John Calvin suffered physical torments. When in the midst of such difficulties, we may doubt God's love for us.

This is why it's so vital for us to separate our feelings from facts that we know to be true. *Feeling* unloved when in fact you are loved more than you can possibly imagine is a matter of correcting your perception. When Scripture states factually that you are loved and you feel otherwise, it's necessary for you to focus on what you know to be true so that your feelings can come into alignment with reality. As theologian Lewis Sperry Chafer observed, "The possession of the indwelling Son of God is the abiding fact of the newly created life in Him, and should never be confused with some imperfect and changeable experience in the daily life."[1] Does it make any sense for us to rely on what our mercurial, untrustworthy feelings might tell us when we have already been given the absolute promises of God regarding the assurance of His unchanging and eternal love for us?

The God of Love

When God says He loves you, this isn't just some vague claim made from billions of miles away in heaven. No, God cares for you deeply and is present with you. Every single hair on your head is numbered (Matthew 10:30), and there is concrete historic proof of His great love, which was expressed at Calvary. The One who counts and calls the stars by name and who numbers the hairs of your head—and who gave His only Son so you could be with Him forever—is never in danger of forgetting the love He has for you.

What's more, God loved you as a sinner. He loved you even when you were unlovable, when you refused to show love to Him:

> God *demonstrates* his own love for us in this: While we were still sinners, Christ died for us (Romans 5:8).

> God *showed how much he loved us* by sending his one and
> only Son into the world so that we might have eternal life
> through him. This is real love—not that we loved God,
> but that he loved us and sent his Son as a sacrifice to take
> away our sins (1 John 4:9-10 NLT).

In addition, because "God is love" (1 John 4:8,16), He can't do anything else *but* love His adopted and redeemed children because it's impossible for Him to do otherwise. When we finally get to heaven, we will understand at last how God worked through the difficult circumstances of life for our good, and how He was loving us even when it seemed otherwise. Again, God can't ever love us more than He does now, or less than He always has. Nor can His love for us ever change. God tells every one of His adopted children that no matter what their circumstances or feelings, "I have loved you with an everlasting love; I have drawn you with unfailing kindness" (Jeremiah 31:3).

Loved Infinitely

Among the more amazing passages in the Bible are two that teach us that *Jesus* loves *us* as much as God the Father loves *Him* (infinitely), and that God the *Father* loves *us* as much as He loves *Jesus* (infinitely):

> I have loved you even as the Father has loved me. Remain
> in my love (John 15:9 NLT).

> You [the Father] love them as much as you love me (John
> 17:23 NLT).

Think about it: How much does God the Father love His precious Son Jesus Christ? That's how much Jesus loves *you*—and that's how much the Father loves *you*.

Consider this as well: If the indescribable agony Jesus suffered upon the cross of Calvary is an expression of the degree of God's love for you, it must be a pretty remarkable love. And the implications of such a great love are staggering:

God raised us up with Christ and seated us with him in the heavenly realms in Christ Jesus, in order that in the coming ages he might show the incomparable riches of his grace, expressed in his kindness to us in Christ Jesus (Ephesians 2:6-7).

I consider that our present sufferings are not worth comparing with the glory that will be revealed in us (Romans 8:18).

No eye has seen...ear has heard...no mind has conceived the things God has prepared for those who love him (1 Corinthians 2:9)[2]

Nothing in all creation will ever be able to separate us from the love of God that is revealed in Christ Jesus our Lord (Romans 8:39 NLT).

As James Smith wrote in *The Love of Christ!*:

Love in *us*—rules us; just so, the infinite love of Jesus, rules Him. All that He has ever *purposed, promised,* or *performed* for His people—has flowed from this *ocean of divine love!* He is a *globe* of love—without beginning or end! He is a *sea* of love—without fault or defect! Only an infinite intellect can grasp Christ's love—only eternity is sufficient to reveal it to our minds. Christ's love will be always *unfolding*—but never be fully unfolded. It will be always *displaying*—but never be fully displayed. We may stand in the center and endeavor to follow its lines—but Christ's love defies our powers, and drowns our thoughts in its immensity! Christ's love can never be *diverted* from its objects; it is *immutably fixed* upon them—and remains fixed forever![3]

Trusting God's Love

If we trust in God's love for us, it solves all kinds of problems. (And if we have difficulty with that, we can pray and ask God to help us believe His promises and give us the personal awareness of His love and His assurance.)

If we trust in God's love, then we can have confidence that everything that comes into our lives—including suffering, adversity, and evil—has been allowed by God for our higher eternal good. Even Jesus Himself, God incarnate, "learned obedience through what he suffered" (Hebrews 5:8 ESV). Consider the trials, miseries, tragedies, and persecutions in the lives of Joseph, King David, Job, or Daniel, as well as Christian martyrs too numerous to mention over the 2000-year history of the church. No matter what the extent of the evil we experience, God is able to work through it to bring about a greater good.[4]

That's not to say everything *is* good; rather, God will *work everything out* for good. How many times have you heard a Christian say the following about some horrible tragedy? "Looking back, I'm actually *glad* it happened because of everything good that came from it."

One great example is the fact the best thing to have ever happened in human history was brought about by the worst thing to have ever happened in human history. The best thing—which is the forgiveness of sins and the free gift of eternal life—came through the worst thing, which was the unjust and horrific killing of Jesus Christ. Yet Jesus' crucifixion was predestined by God because of His great love for us (Acts 2:23; Acts 4:26-28; see also John 3:16).

The Fear of Love?

Strangely, the enormity and extent of God's love for His own seems to be one of the more difficult things for us as Christians to accept. God has lavished all His infinite love upon us, and yet sometimes we shrink from it. Perhaps it's because we know we are unworthy of such amazing love and grace. Or maybe we have allowed guilt feelings to erect a barrier to God's love. But no matter what the reason, all of them are irrelevant. All through this book, we have seen that He gave His love freely as a gift, made it available to us at great personal cost, and He has placed us into an eternal union with Christ, adopting us as His forever children. We have looked at dozens of Bible passages that give us every reason to have confidence in the assurance of our salvation and eternal destination.

So if you happen to find it difficult to accept God's love, then you can probably expect to lack assurance regarding your salvation. After all, how can you be assured you will go to heaven if you're not even certain God really loves *you*? Again, whether your doubts stem from an overly sensitive conscience, a sense of failure, a lack of awareness about the promises in God's Word, long-standing negative circumstances in your life, or the wiles of the devil, there's no reason to give in to them. God wants His children to have assurance, and He clearly wants us to know just how much He loves us. The evidence we've examined in Scripture should put all our fears to rest. And thankfully, even if we fail to rest confident in His love here on earth, we will know and experience His love forever in heaven—a love and acceptance beyond anything we can imagine.

Letting God Love Us

The whole matter of how much God loves us is not a minor issue. What is at stake is our sense of well-being, our sense of worth in Christ and our confidence, our ability to face trials, our assurance of salvation—and our victory over the devil, who is the last being on earth who wants us to believe God loves us. God's glory itself is at stake. Indeed, the less we believe God loves us, the more the devil can damage us.

Conversely, if we accept what Scripture declares about how much God loves us—regardless of our feelings or circumstances—and allow Him to love us, then we will have peace and confidence at all times no matter how difficult life gets. And the best way to build up our assurance of God's love for us is to get to know His person, His work, and His promises. The more we know about who God is and what He has done for us, the more we are able to resist doubts about His love.

Remember, God's love for us goes all the way back into eternity past, as confirmed by Ephesians 1:3-5, and will continue all the way into eternity future. As Psalm 103:17 says, "From *everlasting to everlasting* the Lord's love is with those who fear him."

If past events, whether circumstances or bad choices, have led to doubt or guilt, keep in mind that what has happened before now is water under the bridge. It is forever gone, and there is nothing you can do about it except apply the apostle Paul's exhortation in Philippians 3:13-14: "One thing I do: forgetting what lies behind and reaching forward to what lies ahead, I press on toward the goal for the prize of the upward call of God in Christ Jesus" (Philippians 3:13-14 NASB).

Ultimately we have two choices: We can look upward to a loving God of infinite perfection who loves us beyond measure and who can be trusted beyond measure. Or we can look outward at difficult circumstances or inward to a fallen heart of sin and deception. Where we look will make a real difference in how we live. God has already won all battles (John 14:27; 16:33; 1 Corinthians 15:57; Romans 8:37; 1 John 5:4; Revelation 21:4). Remember—even "if our hearts condemn us, we know that God is greater than our hearts, and he knows everything" (1 John 3:20). And "who shall bring any charge against God's elect? It is God who justifies" (Romans 8:33 ESV). As Psalm 103:10 says, "He does not treat us as our sins deserve or repay us according to our iniquities" (Psalm 103:10).

The apostle Paul gives us this wonderful advice in Colossians 3:1-4:

> Since you have been raised to new life with Christ, set your sights on the realities of heaven, where Christ sits in the place of honor at God's right hand. Think about the things of heaven, not the things of earth. For you died to this life, and your real life is hidden with Christ in God. And when Christ, who is your life, is revealed to the whole world, you will share in all his glory (NLT).

His Love Endures Forever

God loves us with a genuine, unconditional, self-sacrificial love. And in Psalm 136, we are told no less than 26 times that "His love endures forever." The Hebrew word translated "love" is *hesed*, or faithful love. To be sure, if His love endures *forever*, what else could it be but *faithful?* And we find plenty more such assurances in the Psalms:

> *Psalm 100:5*—"The Lord is good and his love endures forever; his faithfulness continues through all generations."
>
> *Psalm 107:1*—"Give thanks to the Lord, for he is good! His faithful love endures forever" (NLT).
>
> *Psalm 117:2*—"Great is his love toward us, and the faithfulness of the Lord endures forever. Praise the Lord."

In these and many other passages that proclaim the faithfulness of God's love, nothing is ever mentioned about our feelings or sin or circumstances ever changing God's love for us. Psalm 89:2 emphatically declares, "Your unfailing love will last forever. Your faithfulness is as enduring as the heavens." Do you believe that? Let the truths of Scripture settle any doubts you might have. Let them fill you with the freedom and joy God wants for you!

What Will Heaven Be Like? Part 1

I believe with all my heart that in order to be useful in
this world we must fall in love with another world.[1]

JOHN PIPER

The concept of heaven (or some idea of the afterlife) is universal among people. It's prevailed throughout all history and in all cultures, having been placed intuitively into the heart of all people by God Himself.[2] As a leading scholarly secular text on heaven observes, "In the ancient world, belief in life after death was widespread, considered normal, and not generally weakened by skepticism."[3] This makes sense, for the Bible tells us that God has placed the knowledge of Himself within all people: "What may be known about God is *plain to them*, because *God has made it plain to them*" (Romans 1:19). This divine declaration does not exclude humanists, secularists, atheists, and skeptics in general. Indeed, God has been their personal teacher. Their suppression of their awareness of God's reality, or their unwillingness to believe, or the brash and hopeless declarations of a few that "there is no God" (Psalm 14:1; 53:1) only reveals little more than their personal bias and their refusal to consider the evidence available to them.

All people know full well that God exists and that they are personally responsible for such knowledge. That is why Romans 1:20 says they are "without excuse" before God. And those who chose to suppress the knowledge of God will eventually come to suffer the consequences that come from their choice to live in unrighteousness (Romans 1:18-32).

Ecclesiastes 3:11 says of people that God has "set eternity in the human heart." That explains every person's intuitive sense of immortality and the universal belief in an afterlife, however perverted it may have become through man-based religions or philosophy.

Of all the world religions, Christianity alone offers people a free and gracious gift of eternal life and a perfect immortality simply on the basis of placing one's personal trust in God the Son, or Jesus Christ. All other religions require people to do good works designed to appease some deity or other. Only Christianity offers an assurance based on what God has done *for* us, instead of calling us to "measure up" to certain expectations or standards that require something *from* us.

The Greatest Disconnect?

Apart from God Himself,[4] heaven is the most dominant, amazing, wonderful, and desirable reality in the whole universe. Yet oddly, heaven is also the most maligned and ignored reality on earth, even among Christians! One modern authority on heaven, Randy Alcorn, is correct when he says that lack of concentration on and appreciation for heaven may be the single greatest weakness of the Western church itself (a reflection of the church's disinterest in theology and apologetics generally—see Hosea 4:6).[5] Why would disinterest in heaven be so consequential? Because to the same extent that we are heavenly minded, we cannot be earthly minded. Put another way, to the extent that we ignore heaven, we are friends with the world—and therefore enemies of God (see James 4:4; 1 John 2:15).

Perhaps that is why Colossians 3:1 urges us, "Set your hearts on things above" (Colossians 3:1). The Greek term translated "set your hearts on" is *zēteite*, which means to seek or seek after, search for, desire, inquire of, keep trying to obtain, or strive for (knowledge of). Alcorn summarizes it as "a diligent, active, single-minded investigation" or pursuit of.[6]

That should be every Christian's attitude toward heaven. Why?

Because, as the late A.W. Tozer observed, "It may be said with certainty that Christians who have lost their enthusiasm about the Savior's promises of heaven-to-come have also stopped being effective in Christian life and witness in this world."[7] That's the last thing on earth any Christian should want, but Tozer is correct: There is a direct correlation between our interest in heaven and our effectiveness in living the Christian life.

That is why knowing about and concentrating upon heaven is to be one of the major priorities in a believer's life. And surely it explains the reason Paul prayed, on behalf of the Christians in Ephesus, "that the eyes of your heart may be enlightened in order *that you may know* the hope to which he has called you, the riches of his glorious inheritance in his holy people" (Ephesians 1:18).

Heaven a Boring Place?

The common caricature of heaven is that it will be a boring place where people sit around worshiping God and playing harps for all eternity. But any such thought is flat-out wrong. The worship of God is boring? Anyone who has even a small idea of who the true God is could hardly entertain that perspective for a moment. (If your ideas of what worship will be like in heaven are based on boring church services, then you've experienced a poor foretaste of what is to come. Don't let weak earthly examples shape your perceptions of the wonders that await us in eternity.)

Consider this matter for a moment from an earthly perspective. Reflect upon the thrill that music can bring to our hearts—a feeling that all of us know full well. For example, ponder the majesty, splendor, and power of Handel's transcendental "Hallelujah Chorus." Or Luciano Pavarotti or The Tenors' hauntingly beautiful rendition of the finale of Puccini's romantic aria "Nessum Dorma," to name just two of many possible examples. Now imagine listening to such music in a setting many times greater than any here on earth.

That might give you a very small glimpse what it will be like to worship God throughout eternity. Countless millions of redeemed people, along with a vast host of angels, will sing together in praise before the infinite glory of the awe-inspiring God whose beauty is indescribable, whose presence is overwhelmingly lovely. The setting will be breathtaking and spectacular beyond words. Boring? Anything but. With eternal creativity, innovation, adventure, excitement, fascination, and rejoicing all a part of everything we do in the presence of an incredible God who loves us infinitely, who could possibly be bored?

How can we assume that the same God who gave us the wonderful gift of music is somehow going to give His children a humdrum, boring existence in heaven for all eternity? What a silly thought. If anything, God will have to "power us down," so to speak, because we will be so eager to worship Him. And even after trillions of years in God's loving and glorious presence, we will have only scratched the surface of all that eternity offers. If we were to attempt to communicate how wonderful heaven will be by saying that it's a thousand times better than the best experience anyone has ever had—or by saying that one second in heaven is better than the most wonderful experiences in a thousand lifetimes—we would still fall immeasurably short of conveying just how great heaven will be.

God—the Greatest Treasure in the Universe

As amazing as heaven is and will be, it is nothing compared to God Himself. Heaven is, after all, a created place, and there is an infinite difference in nature between the Creator and anything created. What will make heaven so special is the presence of God Himself. In other words, if we were to remove God from heaven, then heaven—no matter how perfect it is—would suffer immeasurably.

Consider the following words from pastor and author John Piper, which can be applied not only to our massive hundred-billion light-year physical universe, but to the spiritual universe as well—in fact to all creation visible and invisible:

God's absolute being means all the universe is by comparison to God as nothing. Contingent, dependent reality
is to absolute, independent reality as a shadow to sub-
stance. As an echo to a thunderclap. As a bubble to the
ocean. All that we see, all that we are amazed by in the
world and in the galaxies is, compared to God, as nothing. "All the nations are as nothing before Him, they
are accounted by Him as less than nothing and empti-
ness" (Isaiah 40:17, ESV)....God's absolute being means
that He is the most important and most valuable reality
and the most important and most valuable person in the
universe. He is more worthy of interest and attention
and admiration and enjoyment than all other realities,
including the entire universe....Being the most signifi-
cant reality there is, nothing is rightly known apart from
its relationship to Him. He is the source and goal and
definer of all beings and all things.[8]

Yet *this* infinitely amazing Being is the very One we will explore
forever in a relationship of love for all eternity!

Unfortunately, most people—and this includes many Christians—don't get very excited about the thought of praising and
worshiping God forever because they don't really understand the
wonderful treasure that He is. But try to imagine being in the presence of a personal-triune God of infinite love, joy, pleasure, and creativity. Wouldn't that be amazing? Further, if the cross of Calvary is
an expression of the greatness of God's love, what should we think all
eternity will be like?

What's more, the purpose of heaven is for us to glorify God forever because it is in glorifying God that we receive our greatest joy, and
joy is the business not only of this life but of heaven itself. When we
glorify God, we find our greatest joy because glorifying God and our
greatest joy are really one and the same thing. The reason that God
is supremely concerned with His glory is not only because it is morally right, but because He is infinitely perfect. It follows that for Him

to be less concerned for His glory would be for His creatures (us) to suffer immeasurably.

Thus, as the Westminster catechism says, "The chief end of man is to glorify God *and* enjoy Him forever." We see how God's glory and our joy come together in these words from Amy Plantinga Pauw:

> Because "heaven is a progressive state," the heavenly joy of the saints, and even of the triune God, will forever continue to increase...Saints can look forward to an unending expansion of their knowledge and love of God, as their capacities are stretched by what they receive...There is no intrinsic limit to their joy in heaven...As the Saints continue to increase in knowledge and love of God, God receives more and more glory. This heavenly reciprocity will never cease, because the glory God deserves is infinite, and the capacity of the saints to perceive God's glory and praise him for it is ever increasing.[9]

Enjoying the Creator, Not the Creation

Ironically, to their own detriment, many people focus their time and energy on enjoying *what* God has made (the gift) rather than the One *who* has made it (the Giver). As we've seen, the Giver is infinitely greater and more enjoyable than the gift. To neglect or ignore God is probably one of the greatest crimes in the universe—not giving Him the time of day, never thanking Him, and treating Him with contempt at the same time we enjoy all the good and wonderful gifts He has given us. We greedily grab all the gifts we can, while we ignore the Giver. Unfortunately, of course, we are all God-ignorers and God-demeaners to some extent in this life; but thankfully, that will never again be true of us in heaven—just the opposite.

Nothing greater can or ever could be conceived than the biblical God, because infinite perfection can never be perfected upon. God's infinite perfection is immortal, extending from eternity past throughout eternity future.

The Astounding Increase

One of the most amazing aspects of our future in heaven is that our knowledge of God will likely *increase* forever! Eternity will never end, and therefore its many pleasures will never end. This is one of the mind-blowing realities of heaven—words cannot adequately explain how incredible an experience heaven will be for us. Remember, we are finite beings and always will be; yet God is infinite and always will be.

The fact we will always be learning more about God, who is infinitely perfect, loving, creative, and wonderful, cannot help but continually increase the joy we will know in heaven. And our increased joy cannot help but increase our love for God and our desire to know more about Him—not to mention our love and appreciation for our personal, eternal redemption.[10]

As Sam Storms says, "There will always be more to see when we look at God, because His infinite character can never be exhausted. We could—and will—spend countless millennia exploring the depth of God's being and be no closer to seeing it all than when we first started. This is the magnificence of God and the wonder of heaven."[11] Storms says our relationship with God "will deepen and develop, intensify and amplify, unfold and increase, broaden and balloon" forever.[12]

We like the way Storms puts it in the extended passage cited below:

> Heaven is not simply about the reality or experience of joy, but its eternal increase. The blessedness of the beauty of heaven is progressive, incremental and incessantly expansive...There will not be in heaven a one-time momentary display of God's goodness, but an everlasting, ever-increasing infusion and impartation of His kindness that intensifies with every passing moment...Throughout the ages to come, we will be the recipients of an ever-increasing and more stunning, more fascinating and thus inescapably more enjoyable display of God's saving grace and kindness in Christ than before. We will see and savor

and be increasingly enthralled with fresh displays of His redeeming love. The knowledge we gain when we enter heaven will forever grow and deepen and expand and intensify.

We will constantly be more amazed by God, more in love with God and thus evermore relishing His presence and our relationship with Him. Our experience of God will never reach a consummation or become stale. It will deepen and develop, intensify and amplify—and will reach a crescendo that will even then be only the beginning of an eternity of new and intriguing insights into the majesty of who God is...if our ideas and thoughts of God increase in heaven, then so also must the joy and delight which those ideas and thoughts generate. With increased knowledge comes intensified affection and fascination. With each new insight comes more joy, which serves only to stoke the fires of adoration and celebration around the throne of the Lamb.[13]

And that only scratches the surface of how wonderful heaven will be. There is more that God's children have to look forward to—much more.

What Will Heaven Be Like? Part 2

I pray also that the eyes of your heart may be enlightened in
order that you may know the hope to which he has called
you, the riches of his glorious inheritance in his holy people.

EPHESIANS 1:18

In no other religion in the world does love play the dominant role
that it does in biblical Christianity. Only biblical Christianity has
a God of self-sacrificial love, who "is love" (John 3:16; 1 John 4:8,16)
and who has revealed a religion of self-sacrificial love (1 Corinthians
13:4-7; Ephesians 5:1-2; Philippians 2:1-8).

As Jonathan Edwards points out in his book *Heaven, a World of*
Love, wherever we turn our eyes in heaven we will also behold the
most perfect love imaginable between God, the angels, and the saints.
No matter where we gaze in rapt wonder, we will see bounteous love
and glory and beauty and dignity and joy. "Everyone shall be perfectly
pure and perfectly lovely in heaven." Love will be perfectly given and
perfectly received, always and forever.

Even more amazing is the fact every occupant of heaven will experience an eternal influx of love from the Trinity itself. As the immeasurable love of God involves exercising "an eternal, mutual, holy
energy"[1] of infinite love between members of the Trinity, inflowing
and outflowing forever, *it will not then be confined to the members of the*
Trinity. Once all the redeemed are in heaven, such love will be mani-
fested fully and finally forever. Edwards says, "It flows out [from the
Trinity] in innumerable streams toward all the created inhabitants of
heaven, to all the saints and angels there."[2]

Everyone will love everyone perfectly for all eternity. Each person in heaven will not only constantly and eternally be loved and happy; they will also rejoice in everyone else's happiness and pleasure. The desire for love will never fail to be satisfied, and every redeemed saint will know with the absolute certainty that God's love for them will continue forever. And it gets even better:

> The love of God and Christ for us will be immeasurably beyond the love of the greatest of saints for us and we will increasingly learn about that love forever, worlds without end and see it palpably and visibly displayed to us in wonder after wonder. All the love we experience in heaven, whether from God, the saints or the angels will never be interrupted or diminished, or hindered or withdrawn for any reason, or corrupted in any way but only be fully and perfectly expressed, yea, in a manner unfathomable, increased forever.[3]

Arthur W. Pink wrote an article called "The hell of hell" in which he pointed out the meaning of his title—that after millions and millions of years of perfectly just punishment for sin upon the unredeemed, hell will barely have begun. The opposite is true for heaven, but in a much greater sense. After millions and millions of years in heaven experiencing pleasures, blessings, and wonders beyond what we can imagine, not only will they increase, but even after all that time, heaven will barely have begun—*and it will always be so*.

Imagine what a God of infinite perfection, creativity, wisdom, love, and joy—a God who loves to give everything good to His children—might have in store for His people throughout the ongoing ages and endless millenniums of eternity. To reemphasize the heaven reality: Millions of years can be multiplied times millions of years and eternity will barely have started—*and it will always be so*.

Nevertheless, one would think that after so many eons of increased knowledge, joy, and love that we would virtually explode from the ecstasy; but no, the increase of blessedness will go on forever. Every good thing that is possible to increase forever must be increased forever because it will bring glory to God, and that is the highest good. Despite the difficulty of comprehending such a reality, this truth is accepted and discussed by theologians and Bible scholars such as Jonathan Edwards, John Piper, Sam Storms and others.

And we find affirmation for all this in Scripture as well:

> God raised us up with Christ and seated us with him in the heavenly realms in Christ Jesus, in order that in the coming ages he might show the incomparable riches of his grace, expressed in his kindness to us in Christ Jesus (Ephesians 2:6-7).

> Our light and momentary troubles are achieving for us an eternal glory that far outweighs them all (2 Corinthians 4:17).

> No eye has seen…no ear has heard…no human mind has conceived the things God has prepared for those who love him (1 Corinthians 2:9)[4]

Derivatives and the Real Thing

Randy Alcorn observes that "seeing God will be like seeing everything else for the first time. Our primary joy in heaven will be knowing and seeing God. Every other joy will be derivative, flowing from the fountain of our relationship with God."[5] This is a fundamental and crucial thought—that *everything* originates with and from the absolutely sovereign God, "who alone is immortal" (1 Timothy 6:16). *Everything* is derivative. Everything good we experience in this life was created by God, and created for our enjoyment and happiness specifically because it makes *God* happy and brings *Him* delight and joy. God's love is the source of all lesser love; His beauty the source of all lesser beauty, and so on.

Anything that is good, pleasant, exciting, fun, thrilling—such as joy, love, sex, playfulness, happiness, creativity, adventure, and anything else that is wonderful, fascinating, delightful, refreshing, enjoyable, and so on—is derived ultimately from God. After all, who made all these and much more? God Himself. He created them first—for us. He is the source of everything good (James 1:17). And here's the point: The fact everything else is derivative means that God is the infinitely unique and original nonderivative. He comprises the ultimate source of and the best of everything good in this life, to the most supreme degree.

> All secondary joys are *derivative* in nature. They cannot be separated from God. Flowers are beautiful for one reason—God is beautiful. Rainbows are stunning because God is stunning. Puppies are delightful because God is delightful. Sports are fun because God is fun. Study is rewarding because God is rewarding. Work is fulfilling because God is fulfilling.[6]

Because everything in heaven but God is a secondary joy, the ultimate joy will be God Himself. Just as God "*is* love" (1 John 4:8,16), it can also be stated He "*is* joy." And being in His presence will be the ultimate experience of love, joy, pleasure, wonder, adventure, and so on. Would a hundred of the best superlatives in any language adequately describe a single day in heaven? We doubt it; but even if they did, they wouldn't come close to describing one day in the presence of God.

Because everything good is derivative, it is from the presence of God alone that we can experience them in and to their fullest capacity. In other words, to be in the direct presence of God is to experience the fullest measure of love, the greatest amount of joy, to see the greatest beauty, to comprehend the greatest wonder, to experience the most sublime peace, and so on. That means that whatever we experience in this life, given this world's fallen state, is at best a tiny foretaste of the joy, beauty, and love to come in eternity. What we know here on earth is but a shadow of what awaits us in heaven.

And even the things of heaven will pale in comparison to the enjoyment of God Himself. That which is created will always pale when set alongside the Creator. Would we prefer to merely look at the famous marble sculpture of King David, or to have Michelangelo himself as our best friend, roommate, and mentor? That gives some idea of how wonderful it will be to live in God's presence.

God Delights in Giving

In the same way that parents delight in bringing joy to their children, God will delight in our joy as well. As mind-boggling as it is, we're told that God Himself will actually sing over us!

> He will take great delight in you, in his love he will no longer rebuke you, but will rejoice over you with singing (Zephaniah 3:17).

> The LORD will take delight in you…as a bridegroom rejoices over his bride, so will your God rejoice over you (Isaiah 62:4-5).

As the giver of all things good, and as one who delights in His children, God will bestow upon us an inexhaustible love and everything that is good for us. The gifts He bears for us will never stop coming but will continue for all eternity. Romans 8:32 asks this about God: "He who did not spare his own Son, but gave him up for us all— how will he not also, along with him, graciously give us all things?" (Romans 8:32). God the Father's infinitely precious Son is the greatest gift He could ever have given. And we are told God will go over and above that, and "graciously give us *all* things." That includes everything God has created or will create.

Look at what the Bible says about God's giving nature:

> God…richly provides us with everything for our enjoyment (1 Timothy 6:17).

> You open your hand and satisfy the desires of every living thing (Psalm 145:16).

> Every good and perfect gift is from above, coming down
> from the Father of the heavenly lights (James 1:17).

> They feast on the abundance of your house; you give
> them drink from your river of delights. For with you is
> the fountain of life (Psalm 36:8-9).

Think about how much pleasure we derive from giving good things to our family members, friends, and others. Giving brings great joy; it's part of how God created us. What's more, the Lord Jesus Himself said: "It is more blessed to give than to receive" (Acts 20:35). Being that we are created in God's image, we have some idea of the joy He derives from giving. But with God, we have to expand the giving to infinite dimensions and make it of eternal duration.

One reason God decided to create in the first place was so that He could express the entirety of His infinitely perfect and glorious character, including expressing His love in giving gifts—the greatest being His Son. Given what the Bible tells us about God, it's clear He receives great pleasure from loving and giving, which explains why He will do it forever. In other words, the redeemed will forever be the objects of God's lavish and extravagant giving. Those who dwell in heaven will be on the receiving end of God's love and joy and be given good and wonderful gifts forever. His giving will never end because eternity will never end, nor will our astonishment and gratefulness over all that He gives us.

The New Jerusalem

Among the gifts we receive will be the New Jerusalem. This dwelling place will be the crown jewel of the universe—that is, of the "new heaven and a new earth" (2 Peter 3:13; Revelation 21:1).

At the beginning of eternity, the New Jerusalem, described in Revelation 21, will come down from heaven and become our new dwelling place. It will be a massive city of pure gold—except pure as glass—shining with the very glory of God. It will be stunning and beautiful beyond comparison. We are told the city will be "laid out like a square (verse 16), or a perfect cube, about 1400 miles in height, width, and depth, or slightly smaller than the size of our moon. That would make the surface area of the New Jerusalem about 2.25 million square miles. For comparison, all of Texas covers 268,000 square miles, and Alaska encompasses 663,000 square miles. The New Jerusalem is far bigger than India, and as large as England 40 times over. If placed in the middle of the United States, it would stretch from Canada to Mexico and from California to Eastern Tennessee. But remember, that's only the ground floor of the New Jerusalem, which will extend 1400 miles into space. That's a massive city!

The New Jerusalem will be a city of incredibly glorious light illuminated in a special way by the infinite glory and light of God Himself (Revelation 21:23). And we can expect this magnificent city to have the most beautiful rivers and waterfalls, trees, mountains, lakes, canyons, plants and animals, architecture, and a culture like none experienced in the history of the earth. Everything about the New Jerusalem will be stunning—most of all God Himself and His Son, who will dwell there personally with us.

Exploration and Adventures

Most of us take pleasure in traveling to exotic and stunningly beautiful places on this earth. Some examples include Maui, Hawaii, consistently voted "the best island in the world"; Lucerne, Switzerland; Venice, Italy; Niagara Falls; the Grand Bahama Island; the Serengeti, Africa; New Zealand's Bay of Islands; the Amazon River or China's Yangtze River; Europe's Mediterranean coast; Tuscany, Italy; or the Maldives in the Indian Ocean. Every one of these is an outstandingly beautiful destination—yet they will all pale in comparison to what will surround us in eternity. Everything in our new home, in every way possible, will reflect God's infinite beauty, infinite wisdom, infinite love. and infinite creativity.

Again, as Randy Alcorn says,

God is a creator. He'll never stop being what He is. We should expect new and wondrous creations that declare His glory. God hasn't exhausted His creative resources. He never will.

> ...should it surprise us if God creates the substance of which science fiction, fantasy, and mythology are but shadows?...God has given us a longing for new worlds...Considering that His higher glory and praise comes not from inanimate objects such as stars and planets but from intelligent being such as people and angels, it's no great stretch to suppose He might create other intelligent beings...I anticipate an eternity of delight in watching and discovering what He creates to reveal more of Himself to us.[7]

Ephesians 3:20 reminds us that God "is able to do immeasurably more than all we ask or imagine" (Ephesians 3:20). That being true, where are the limits to what we might expect in eternity?

And because everything God does will be for and to display His eternal, infinite glory, whatever He does will be the best He can do and give. Yet even then, everything that surrounds us for all eternity will still pale in comparison to the wonder of God's actual presence. Imagine sitting down and having a conversation with God, your best friend in the universe, the one who always has and always will love you, in person, anytime you want, on any subject you can think of! Imagine Him creating gifts just for you, perfectly fitting your interests, tastes, and personality, for no other reason than for you to enjoy them, have fun with them, and rejoice over them.

Even more wonderful is that God will have designed everything throughout eternity to help us see and know *Him* better and better, to understand Him in greater ways, to glorify Him more and more—the totality of which will bring us ever-increasing happiness and joy. Every adventure and exploration will tell us more about God, revealing something special—some new intriguing facet of His infinitely perfect nature and glory, some incredible insight into His infinitely complex personality, some new wonder of His infinite love, some awesome spectacle of His infinite beauty. And thus everything we do and see throughout time without end will only motivate and excite us to explore yet more and more of all that He is and to love Him more and more for the unending and immeasurable treasure that He always remains.

And yet it gets even better. We don't just have one infinite Person to explore and love and worship and wonder on forever; we actually have three infinite Persons—God the Father, God the Son, and God the Holy Spirit. We'll have infinite diversity. And so the reservoir of things to do will never run dry but be replenished daily and expanded onto all of eternity in ever new and astonishing ways. We will be utterly fascinated with God forever, even as the angels have already been for millennia.

In the midst of marveling over all this heavenly splendor we must remember that we will finally be without sin. And we will have perfect health. We will not have imperfections or disabilities of any kind. As 1 Corinthians 15:53 says, "The perishable must clothe itself with the imperishable, and the mortal with immortality." Nothing from this fallen world will impede upon or impair our ability to enjoy the fullness of God Himself and all that He has to offer us. The joys we know right now will be magnified many times over because we will experience them in perfect bodies.

Like Jesus

That leads us to our next point: One of the greatest things about heaven is that we won't just be resurrected from the dead—we will be *like* Jesus. We currently have little idea of what this means: "Dear friends, now we are children of God, and what we will be has not yet been made known. *But we know that when Christ appears, we shall be like him, for we shall see him as He is*" (1 John 3:2). Our resurrection bodies will be unlike anything we can imagine—there will be continuity with what we are now, but for all intents and purposes we will be supernatural beings.

For example, might we be able to travel at the speed of thought? Or we fly through the air like an eagle? Whatever the case, our bodies will be made specifically for experiencing and worshiping God (which will give us the greatest pleasure possible) and for experiencing the new heavens and the new earth. We will always be discovering new things and always be surprised and delighted by God's new creation and the things He gives to us.

All of what we've talked about in the last two chapters is a mere speck of the reality we will know in heaven. Again, as 1 Corinthians 2:9 says, "no human mind has conceived what God has prepared for those who love him." We who are Christians have an incredible future awaiting us.

The most important message of all in this book is that you make certain that you are going to heaven. Make sure you have truly trusted Jesus Christ to forgive your sins and believed on Him for eternal life. If you haven't yet done so, give Him your life today.

God so loved the world that he gave his one and only Son,
that whoever believes in him shall not perish
but have eternal life (John 3:16).

Recommended Reading

Burk Parsons, ed., *Assured by God: Living in the Fullness of God's Grace* (Phillipsburg, NJ: P&R Publishing, 2007). A worthwhile collection of essays by R. Albert Mohler, Jr., Sinclair B. Ferguson, John MacArthur, Jerry Bridges, R.C. Sproul, and more.

Erwin W. Lutzer, *How You Can Be Sure That You Will Spend Eternity with God* (Chicago: Moody, 1996). A short and simple book, highly readable.

Lewis Sperry Chafer, *Systematic Theology, Volume III: Soteriology* (salvation) (Dallas: Dallas Seminary Press, 1948). This provides a more detailed look at the breadth of biblical salvation.

About the Authors

John Ankerberg, host of the award-winning John Ankerberg Show, has three earned graduate degrees: an MA in church history and the philosophy of Christian thought, an MDiv from Trinity Evangelical Divinity School, and a DMin from Luther Rice Seminary. He has authored, coauthored, or edited more than 90 books, including the two-million-selling "Facts On" series of apologetic books and *Middle East Meltdown*.

John Weldon has seven earned degrees, including master's degrees in divinity and Christian apologetics, and a doctorate in comparative religion, and has authored or coauthored more than 100 books and 200 articles.

For more information, please visit our website at
http://www.jashow.org.

Notes

Where Will You Spend Eternity?

1. Erwin W. Lutzer, *How You Can Be Sure That You Will Spend Eternity with God* (Chicago: Moody, 1996), 27.

Chapter 1—How Do You Know?

1. R.T. Kendall, *Understanding Theology*, vol. 1 (Scotland: Christian Focus, 2002), 158.

2. Sam Storms, *Pleasures Forevermore* (Colorado Springs: NavPress, 2000), 42-43.

3. An otherwise excellent and highly recommended article analyzing the "free grace" and "Lordship salvation" positions: M. James Sawyer, "Some Thoughts on Lordship Salvation" May 25, 2004, available at Bible.org; http://bible.org/article/some-thoughts-lordship-sal vation, originally delivered November 1990 at the Evangelical Theological Society annual meeting in Kansas City, Missouri. As an illustration, Dr. Sawyer argues that it is impossible to posit "ideal mathematical certainty for an internal psychological reality." However, does this category of certainty per se necessarily have the ability to countermand the promises of God when it comes to offering people 100 percent assurance of heaven? What if psychological assurance is a gift of the Holy Spirit? The highest level of truth must lie within God—e.g., that which is declared to be true within the interpersonal communication of the members of the Godhead, which has nothing to do with human psychology. This "theological certainty" (if we may use such a term) would constitute a level of mathematical certainty or greater. What, then, would be the contingencies to qualify divine promises when they are psychologically accepted as fully true? Granted, our psychological reality in relationship to 1 John 5:13 isn't the same as the "ideal world" of mathematical certainty—but what about one Person of the Godhead speaking to another Person of the Godhead about our assurance of salvation as in John 17:2-3,6-12,17,20-24? What if Jesus is speaking of His relationship with the Father in such a manner that He is including His relationship with the believer as in John 10:14-15,27-30? How does mediation or perception through fallen psychological reality necessarily and universally reduce the assurance? Why isn't it possible that the third Person of the Godhead could not give believers 100 percent assurance of salvation equivalent to mathematical certainty? Isn't it logical to assume that declarations made solely between the Father and the Son (declarations that represent promises of 100 percent assurance of salvation to the believer) would have an equivalent or even higher level of certainty than mathematical certainty?

But if so, what of the, in effect, infinitely authoritative and infinitely certain declarations of God the Son alone speaking to us in His promises about our assurance of salvation (e.g., John 5:24; 6:47; 10:30-33)? Would these not be considered 100 percent certain, even though mediated psychologically? It doesn't seem to make sense for God to desire that the certainty be one-sided (from the perspective of His side alone) when He has chosen to communicate His absolute truth to us even though mediated psychologically. Could God's Word ever have *less* assurance than mathematical certainty, assuming the psychological capacity to grasp and accept its truth? Can the promises of an infinite, immutable, truthful God, even in a fallen, imperfect world, have *less* certainty than a mathematical equation? This would not mean everyone may now acquire perfect assurance at every moment throughout their life, because faith does waver and spiritual warfare is a deadly serious reality.

But we believe such 100 percent assurance is possible throughout the large majority of life for anyone who trusts God's salvation, character, and promises. After all, if assurance is declared to be less than 100 percent based on various categories of certainty, then just how much less is it and what is the highest possible level we can ever arrive at, and how do we know? Also, if it is less than 100 percent, it simply isn't full assurance and genuine assurance is no longer possible, something contradicted by the Word of God. We agree with Dr. Bob Wilkin, who logically maintains that "unless Scripture gives some reason why 100% assurance is only for select people—and no such reason is given, it must be available to all…According to the apostle John in 1 John 5:13 it is the birthright of every believer to know with certainty—not to guess or have some degree of confidence—that he or she is eternally secure. If one is not 100% certain of this, then he does not have assurance of salvation." (Bob Wilkin, "Assurance: That You May Know" (condensed version of a paper given November 16, 1990 at the annual Evangelical Theological Society meetings in New Orleans; <http://www.faithalone.org/magazine/y1990/90dec2.html>).

4. The use of the word *faith* in 1 Peter 1:5 does not involve any doubt because faith is a divinely sustained gift. As theologian J.I. Packer observes in his classic, *Knowing God* (Downers Grove, IL: InterVarsity, 1993), page 275: "Your faith will not fail while God sustains it; you are not strong enough to fall away while God is resolved to hold you."

Chapter 2—God's Power and Our Assurance

1. See "Parallel Commentaries: Jamieson-Fausset-Brown Bible Commentary" on Romans 8:31, at http://bible.cc/romans/8-31.htm.

2. R.T. Kendall, *Understanding Theology*, vol. 1 (Scotland: Christian Focus, 2002), 158.

3. John MacArthur, *The Glory of Heaven* (Wheaton, IL: Crossway, 1996), 60-61, emphasis added.

Chapter 3—Assurance That Is 100 Percent or Nothing?

1. See "Parallel Translations: Barnes' Notes on the Bible" on Colossians 2:2 at http://bible.cc/colossians/2-2.htm.

2. Ibid.

3. We are not saying Christians with a less-than-perfect theology can never have personal assurance, for then none would have it. The Holy Spirit can give any believer assurance and has often graciously done so; it is to maintain there is no logical basis for full assurance after the point of regeneration based on what we do as Christians.

4. R.T. Kendall, *Understanding Theology*, vol. 1 (Scotland: Christian Focus, 2002), 158-59.

5. Granted, Calvinists believe the biblical truth that God does the works through us and that He perseveres or preserves the believer to the end, but this is something different than actually looking to those works and perseverance for personal assurance. Ascertaining the quality of those works and whether or not we will persevere (based on election in relation to limited atonement and what might be termed a sense of false election), it becomes impossible to know if we will succeed (given standard post-Calvin "Calvinistic" theology) until the day we die, when it may then be too late.

6. John MacArthur, *The Glory of Heaven* (Wheaton, IL: Crossway, 1996), 120-21.

7. We are not denying biblical teaching on perseverance, only rejecting the idea that it can

become a basis for assurance. Some Christians, looking at their own weakness, worry about persevering in the faith. They never have to: "To *Him* who is *able* to keep you from stumbling and to present you before his glorious presence without fault and with great joy—to the only God our Savior be glory, majesty, power and authority, through Jesus Christ our Lord, before all ages, now and forevermore! Amen" (Jude 24-25).

It is critical that Christians, especially those who have a sensitive nature, realize that "our perseverance" in faith does not ultimately depend upon *our* perseverance in our ability or power. What are we but dust and sin? Perseverance in the faith does not and cannot ultimately depend upon us—it depends upon *God*. If our salvation depended on us, of course it can fail, and would probably fail in every single case. But if salvation and our perseverance depend on God, of course it can never fail. Yes, we exercise personal faith and it may at times vary depending on circumstances and spiritual warfare—our spiritual life may have its hills and valleys, but regardless "it is *God* who works in you to will and to act in order to fulfill his good purpose" (Philippians 2:13). "For we *are God's handiwork*, created in Christ Jesus to do good works, which God prepared in advance for us to do" (Ephesians 2:10). "I am the vine; you are the branches. If you remain in me and I in you, *you will bear much fruit*; apart from me you can do nothing" (John 15:5). "You did not choose me, but I chose you and appointed you that you might go and bear fruit— *fruit that will last*" (John 15:16).

So if we happen to be worried about losing our faith or not persevering, we shouldn't be. A good study of the doctrine of perseverance shows that a genuine faith endures because God Himself maintains it and *causes* it to endure. But even if theoretically for some reason it didn't, once spiritually reborn, a person is saved forever. We agree with Charles Stanley: "Even if a believer for all practical purposes becomes an unbeliever, his salvation is not in jeopardy...believers who lose or abandon their faith will retain their salvation" (*Eternal Security: Can You Be Sure?* [Nashville, TN: Thomas Nelson, 1990], 5). The real question is whether or not a born-again believer *can* actually ever permanently apostatize, and we don't believe they can. Every case I (Weldon) have looked at of professed Christians, including a few professed evangelicals, who have left the faith suggests they were never born again to begin with.

Consider what the Bible teaches about God (not ourselves) causing us to persevere in our faith. Read slowly and consider carefully the following ten verses, which are a sampling of what is found in Scripture:

- "I am *certain* that God, who *began* the good work within you, *will continue his work until it is finally finished* on the day when Christ Jesus returns" (Philippians 1:6 NLT).

- "...to all who have been called by God the Father, who loves you and *keeps you safe in the care of Jesus Christ*" (Jude 1).

- "Father, protect them *by the power of your name*" (John 17:11).

- "Surely God is my help; the LORD *is the one who sustains me*" (Psalm 54:4).

- "He *will guard* the feet of his faithful servants" (1 Samuel 2:9).

- "Do not lack any spiritual gift as you eagerly wait for our Lord Jesus Christ to be revealed. He *will also keep you firm* [other translations read 'sustain you'] *to the end*, so that you will be blameless on the day of our Lord Jesus Christ. *God is faithful, who has called you* into fellowship with his Son, Jesus Christ our Lord" (1 Corinthians 1:7-9).

- "The Lord...*will bring me safely to his heavenly kingdom*. To him be glory for ever and ever. Amen" (2 Timothy 4:18).

- "May the God *who gives endurance* and encouragement give you the same attitude of mind toward each other that Christ Jesus had" (Romans 15:5).

- "May our Lord Jesus Christ himself and God our Father, who loved us and by his grace gave us *eternal encouragement…*" (2 Thessalonians 2:16).
- "The LORD loves the just and will not forsake his faithful ones" (Psalm 37:28).

There are many similar Scripture passages (e.g., Psalm 48:14; 73:24; 91:4; James 2:5), and collectively they are unassailable. How is it possible for God, truthfully and logically, to give believers "eternal encouragement" if there's any chance at all in this life that they will lose their faith irrevocably or go to hell?

Biblically, yes, the genuine believer is characterized by fruit-bearing and continuing faith, which may be one point of the parable of the sower. But it's also true biblically that genuine faith cannot fail because we have been miraculously regenerated and have become new creatures *in* Christ Jesus, already transferred from eternal death to eternal life. We aren't the same; we are truly transformed people with the Holy Spirit Himself indwelling us. If there is no evidence at all of transformation, there's good reason to question the legitimacy of one's faith. But given saving faith, this is why we read airtight passages such as the following:

- "This is the will of him who sent me [God], that I shall *lose none of all those he has given me*, but raise them up at the last day. For my Father's will is that everyone who looks to the Son and believes in him *shall have eternal life, and I will raise them up* at the last day" (John 6:39-40).

- "My sheep listen to my voice; I know them, and they follow me. I *give them eternal life, and they shall never perish*; no one will snatch them out of my hand. My Father, who has given them to me, is *greater than all*; no one can snatch them out of my Father's hand. I and the Father are one" (John 10:27-30).

No less than Augustine declared, "To the saints, perseverance itself is bestowed. They are not only given the gift by the means of which they can persevere; more than that, they are given the gift by means of which they cannot help persevering" (Jerry Bridges, "The Blessing of Discipline" in Burk Parsons (ed.), *Assured by God: Living in the Fullness of God's Grace* [Phillipsburg, NJ: P&R Publishing, 2007], 155. Jonathan Edwards emphasized, "God, in the act of justification, which is passed on a sinner's first believing, has respect to perseverance, as being virtually contained in that first act of faith; and [persevering in faith] is looked upon…as being as it were a property of that [first act of] faith. God has respect to the believer's continuance in faith, and he is justified by that, as though it already were, because by divine establishment it shall follow" (John Piper, "The Purpose and Perseverance of Faith," October 10, 1999, at http://www.desiringgod.org/resource-library/sermons/the-purpose-and-perseverance-of-faith, citing "Justification by Faith Alone," in *The Works of Jonathan Edwards*, vol. 1 [Edinburgh: Banner of Truth Trust, 1974], 641). Piper asserts, "God himself will make sure of our perseverance in faith—not perfection in faith, but perseverance, persistence…This is a very precious truth: that God himself is committed to keeping his own sheep and not letting them forsake him utterly. They may stray for a season. But he will bring them back. Clouds may gather and faith may falter, but those who are justified will not stumble so as to fall utterly. They will persevere in faith. Our hope for glorification is not in our own willpower to believe. It is in God's faithfulness that he who began a good work in us will complete it unto the day of Christ (Philippians 1:6)." John Piper, "The Purpose and Perseverance of Faith." October 10, 1999, at http://www.desiringgod.org/resource-library/sermons/the-purpose-and-perseverance-of-faith.

8. R.T. Kendall, *Why Jesus Died: A Meditation on Isaiah 53* (Oxford, UK: Monarch Books, 2011), 179.

9. R.T. Kendall, *Understanding Theology*, vol. 1 (Scotland: Christian Focus, 2002), 161.

Chapter 4—The Greatest Irony?

1. Randy Alcorn, *Heaven* (Wheaton, IL: Tyndale, 2004), 23; citing the *Los Angeles Times*, October 24, 2003.

2. According to an extensive survey by the Pew Forum on Religion & Public Life, almost 80% of Americans over 18 (78.4%), relying on "self-reported religious identity as the measure of religious affiliation" (Pew Forum on Religion & Public Life, "US Religious Landscape Survey: Summary of Key Findings," survey conducted on a representative sampling of over 35,000 American adults, May 8-August 13, 2007; http://religions.pewforum.org/reports). According to an ABC news poll 83% of Americans identify themselves as Christians, with 37% of them claiming to be "born again." (Gary Langor, "Poll: Most Americans Say They're Christian," ABC News, July 18, 2012 ; poll conducted June 20-24 among a random sampling of 1022 adults; http://abcnews.go.com/US/story?id=90356&page=1#.UESa25bNGSp). According to Gallup, 42% of Americans identify themselves as "born again" or evangelical Christians (Albert L Winseman, DMin, "US Evangelicals: How Many Walk the Walk?" Gallup Commentary, May 31, 2005; http://www.gallup.com/poll/16519/us-evangelicals-how-many-walk-walk.aspx.

   However, the number can go as low as 18-22% depending on the criteria—in this case, sharing their faith in Jesus, believing in biblical inerrancy and having a born-again experience. Gallup polling over the years indicates self-identified evangelical "born again" Christians constituted between 33% and 47% of the US population; 30% would be 80 million people.

3. Much could be said on this point, but consider that those who believe they can lose their salvation generally are assured of their salvation in the moment, but unsure in the long run. Calvinists, who believe the elect cannot lose their salvation (ironically) also often believe they can't personally know if they are elected to eternal life unless their individual sanctification is sufficient and they persevere in the faith and good works until the very end of their lives. In neither case is true assurance possible.

4. R.C. Sproul, *Can I Be Sure I'm Saved?* (Orlando, FL: Ligonier Ministries, 2000), 43-44.

5. Bob Wilkin, "The Fourth Gospel Solves the 'Final Justification' Concern," *Grace in Focus Journal*, March-April 2011; http://www.faithalone.org/magazine/y2011/11B1.html. However, the correctness of Wilkin's assessment depends on the meaning of "believe" in his statement. If it is mental assent alone and not some degree of commitment, there is reason to question assurance on that basis, but his point is still taken: Far too few Christians accept even the possibility of assurance, let alone reality.

6. As to the world, perhaps only the fact of personal pride and spiritual warfare can explain such an oddity, because those who believe they are already going to heaven apart from Christ have no need to do anything else to guarantee they go to hell forever; their default position is fixed regardless of their belief about going to heaven (John 3:36; 2 Corinthians 4:4; Ephesians 2:2) until they trust Christ. As to the church, perhaps this is only a natural resistance to grace without charge based on an assumption that the fact of biblical fruit and perseverance somehow disqualify the possession of assurance; those who believe God sovereignly perseveres the believer and do not look to spiritual performance for assurance would be excepted. In other cases, an Arminian theology or lack of sound theological education may explain missing the mark of assurance.

7. See Matthew 7:13,22-23; John 3:36. An unbeliever's not going to heaven assumes they never personally trusted in Jesus Christ for forgiveness of sins in this life. Any unbeliever can change their eternal destiny in a moment—until it is too late, the point of death (Hebrews 9:27).

Chapter 5—What God Wants Us to Know About Salvation

1. Jerry Trousdale, *Miraculous Movements: How Hundreds of Thousands of Muslims Are Falling in Love with Jesus* (Nashville, TN: Thomas Nelson, 2012), 130.

2. The participle construction of the present tense of "believing on Jesus" in e.g., 1 John 5:10-13 ("whoever believes in the Son of God") tells us that the believer is characterized by believing—but this cannot demand the loss of salvation should the believing theoretically ever cease believing. Those who believe Christians can lose their salvation and go to hell point out that the verb "believe" is a present active participle (John 3:16,36; 5:24; 6:40,47; 11:25). They may cite a reference work such as the well-known *Bible Knowledge Commentary*, which points out, "'He who believes' is in Greek a participial construction in the present tense, meaning that a believer is characterized by his continuing trust." (In 1 John 5:13 "believe" [*pisteuousin*], present participle active, dative masculine plural, currently taking place or taking place repeatedly.)

   But first, Greek tenses never overturn established doctrine.

   Second, the believer being characterized by his or her continuing trust is hardly unexpected for a person who has been spiritually reborn through supernatural power, with the Holy Spirit indwelling them forever and Christ "always living" to intercede for them forever.

   Third, "This is a commonly held fallacy. The Greek present tense does not demand a continuous nuance, but receives its aspect from the context and the nature of the action itself" (J. Kevin Butcher, "A Critique of the Gospel According to Jesus" *Journal of the Grace Evangelical Society*, Spring 1989; http://www.galaxie.com/article/10939).

3. M.R. Vincent, *Word Studies in the New Testament* (Bellingham, WA: Logos Research Systems, 2002), 1 John 5:13, emphasis in original.

4. Kenneth Wuest, *Wuest's Word Studies from the Greek New Testament* (Grand Rapids: Eerdmans, 1997), 1 John 5:13, first emphasis added.

5. Kenneth Wuest, *The New Testament: An Expanded Translation* (Grand Rapids: Eerdmans, 1961), 574.

6. M.S. Heiser, *Glossary of Morpho-Syntactic Database Terminology* (Bellingham, WA: Logos Bible Software, 2005).

7. Words typically have a range of meaning, and this is true for *aion* and a*ionion*, but the modifiers and context make the meaning clear, despite Universalists' dishonesty with these terms. For a critique see Pastor Kerry Kinchen, "Aion Aionios Aionion as Eternal Everlasting Forever," Bridgeway Bible Church, Bulverde, Texas; http://www.bridgewaybiblechurch.com/index.php/sermons/80-aion-and-aionios-as-eternal-everlating-forever/236-aion-aionios-aionion-as-eternal-everlasting-forever. Although I (Weldon) have not read it, the church offers an online book examining all the passages Arminians used to teach the loss of salvation: Kerry Kinchen, *Biblically Defending Salvation*; http://www.bridgewaybiblechurch.com/index.php/biblically-defending-salvation. The book is based on a year-long study that "cover[s] all the main passages in the New Testament that are wrongly interpreted to support the philosophy that salvation is not once for all time, and is able to be lost." In addition see the books in the recommended reading section on page 130 which also cover these passages. See also J.B. Bond, et al, *The Grace New Testament Commentary* (Denton, TX: Grace Evangelical Society, 2010), a "free grace" commentary on the New Testament, which also covers the so-called problem verses.

8. Wayne Gruden, *Systematic Theology* (Grand Rapids: Zondervan, 1994).

9. "Aionios: The NAS New Testament Greek Lexicon" BibleStudyTools.com; http://www.biblestudytools.com/lexicons/greek/nas/aionios.html.

10. For a brief survey see Tom Logan, "'Aionios': a Lexical Survey," Tom Logan Index, 1John57
     .com; http://www.1john57.com/aionios.htm.

Chapter 6—No Middle Ground

1. There isn't a single verse in the Bible that teaches a true Christian can lose their salvation—
    there are only warnings to false professors, warnings about divine discipline, warnings to
    Christians about loss of eternal rewards, or a currently uncertain meaning with several pos-
    sible interpretations. For example, 2 John 9, which says, "Watch yourselves, so that you
    may not lose what we have worked for, but may win a full reward," has to do with eternal
    rewards, and not one's salvation. Biblical and theological scholars throughout the history
    of the church have long maintained that the very idea of "problem passages" is a misno-
    mer based upon the established fact of eternal security and Scripture's inability to contra-
    dict itself. A given passage may not be fully understood, but it can be known with absolute
    certainty what it does not teach: the loss of eternal salvation.
        Joel R. Beeke, president of Puritan Reformed Theological Seminary and professor of
    systematic theology and homiletics, the author or editor of over 50 books and 1500 arti-
    cles, points out that "all ninety-six verses of the warning passages in Hebrews are encour-
    agements to persevere in the faith in the midst of difficulties and discouragement; none
    of them denies perseverance or assurance" (Joel R. Beeke, "The Fullness of Grace" in
    Burk Parsons (ed.), *Assured by God: Living in the Fullness of God's Grace* [Phillipsburg, NJ:
    P&R Publishing, 2006], 119.) In addition, many similar verses may refer to warnings of
    loss of rewards, but none to loss of salvation. As R.T. Kendall concludes, "There is not a
    single verse in the Bible that suggests we can lose our salvation—only our inheritance or
    reward (Colossians 3:24)" (R.T. Kendall, *Understanding Theology*, vol. 1 [Scotland: Chris-
    tian Focus, 2002], 163).

Chapter 7—Who Wants the Joy?

1. Dr. John Piper takes another view in his book *Future Grace*, arguing that gratitude is not
    the basis for moral behavior in the Bible, which he correctly labels "stunning." "...the past-
    orientation of the debtor's ethic tends to blind us to the infinite, never-ending, inexhaust-
    ible, interrupted flow of future grace from this moment to eternity. This grace is there in
    the future to be trusted and lived on. It is there to give the motivation and power for our
    obedience. This infinite overflow of God's grace is dishonored when we fail to appropri-
    ate it by faith in future grace. Gratitude is not designed for this. Faith is." Further, because
    everything works together for our good and we are to give thanks in *all* things and be anx-
    ious for *nothing* (Romans 8:28; Ephesians 5:20; Philippians 4:6, etc.), "only if we trust in
    God to turn past calamities into future comfort can we look back with gratitude for all
    things" (John Piper, *Future Grace*, pp. 47, 49 cf. 33-35, 44). Biblically, I (Weldon) think
    both positions are true.

2. For more on this, see www.DesiringGod.org.

3. Romans 11:36; 16:27; Galatians 1:5; Ephesians 3:21; Philippians 4:20; Colossians 1:16;
    1 Timothy 1:17; 2 Timothy 4:18; Hebrews 13:21; 1 Peter 4:11; 2 Peter 3:18; Jude 25; Reve-
    lation 1:6; 5:13; 7:12.

Chapter 8—Having Eternal Life Now

1. *Play Strindberg,* 7th round (1969).

2. 1 John 3:15:μένουσαν, *Strong's Exhaustive Concordance*; http://concordances.org/strongs/
    greek/3306.htm.

3. This is a paraphrase of the Hebrew *emeth*, truth or faithfulness, as in Psalm 117:2, "He loves us with unfailing love; the Lord's faithfulness endures forever. Praise the Lord!" (NLT). In that whenever God promises us something it must come true, the paraphrase is valid. For God to keep His promises forever is another way to say that God remains faithful forever.

4. Kenneth Wuest, *The New Testament: An Expanded Translation* (Grand Rapids: Eerdmans, 1961), 222.

5. Wuest, *The New Testament: An Expanded Translation*, 239.

6. Kenneth Wuest, *Wuest's Word Studies from the Greek New Testament* (Grand Rapids: Eerdmans, 1997), Ephesians 1:14.

7. Staff, "Topical Studies: Arrabona" Bible Tools; http://www.bibletools.org/index.cfm/fuseaction/Topical.show/RTD/cgg/ID/5953/Arrabona.htm#ixzz25QcWuLhc.

8. Kenneth Wuest, *The New Testament: An Expanded Translation*, 1961, 241, emphasis added.

Chapter 9—What's in a Gift?

1. C.H. Spurgeon, "Praise for the Gift of Gifts," sermon at the Metropolitan Tabernacle, July 27, 1890.

2. See "Gift," http://dictionary.reference.com/browse/gift.

3. Romans 6:23:χάρισμα, *Thayer's Greek Lexicon*; http://concordances.org/thayers/5486.htm.

Chapter 10—What Is the Nature of Saving Faith?

1. John Frame, *Apologetics to the Glory of God: An Introduction* (Phillipsburg, NJ: P&R Publishing, 1994), 81n.

2. Citing Adolf Deissmann in *Light from the Ancient East* (Grand Rapids: Baker, 1978), e.g., 121, 323.

3. M.J. Sawyer, "Some Thoughts on Lordship Salvation," Bible.org, May 25, 2004; http://bible.org/article/some-thoughts-lordship-salvation, cf. H.E. Dana and Julius R. Mantey, *A Manual Grammar of the Greek New Testament* (New York: Macmillian, 1955), 105.

4. Ibid.

5. S. Lewis Johnson Jr., "How Faith Works," *Christianity Today*, July 12, 2012; http://www.christianitytoday.com/ct/2012/julyweb-only/how-faith-works.html?start=3.

6. Ibid; http://www.christianitytoday.com/ct/2012/julyweb-only/how-faith-works.html?start=4.

7. The Greek *teleiótēs*, from *teleioo*, can also be translated as perfecter, accomplisher, or completer.

8. C.H. Spurgeon, The Spurgeon Archive; http://www.spurgeon.org/mainpage.htm.

Chapter 11—What Is the Nature of Eternal Life?

1. John Kohut, "Eternal Life in the Bible," *Grace in Focus Magazine*, March-April 2011; http://www.faithalone.org/magazine/y2011/11B3.html.

2. John F. Walvoord, R.B. Zuck, eds., *The Bible Knowledge Commentary: New Testament Edition* (Wheaton, IL: Victor Books, 1983), John 3:16.

3. John MacArthur, *The Glory of Heaven* Wheaton, IL: Crossway, 1996), 120.

4. Ibid., 61.

5. See http://concordances.org/thayers/2222.htm.

6. See *ATS Bible Dictionary*, "Life"; http://topicalbible.org/l/life.htm.

7. God's incommunicable attributes cannot be communicated, but our union with Christ is more than mere symbolism or metaphor, and it is more than just our "positional" truth considered academically. A different but similar word is found in Hebrews 12:10, where we may be said to partake of the very holiness of God. This union is utterly inseparable— it cannot be broken throughout eternity because we are mysteriously cojoined, integrated, attached, interwoven, and molded together with Christ. To the extent it is possible for a finite being, we are as much a part of Christ as He is a part of the Trinity. The original New Testament Greek word used here, *koinonos*, means partner, companion, share, partaker, fellow-partaker. The Net Bible has a note on this verse pointing out "that believers have an organic connection with God. Because of such a connection, God can truly be called our Father. Conceptually, this bears the same meaning as Paul's 'in Christ' formula..." (Precept Austin Ministries; http://www.preceptaustin.org/2_peter_13-4.htm). C.H. Spurgeon notes, "Moreover, we become partakers of the divine nature in even a higher sense than this—in fact, in as lofty a sense as can be conceived, short of our being absolutely divine. Do we not become members of the body of the divine person of Christ? Yes, the same blood which flows in the head flows in the hand: and the same life which quickens Christ quickens His people, for 'Ye are dead, and your life is hid with Christ in God.' (Col. 3:3-note) Nay, as if this were not enough, we are married unto Christ. He hath betrothed us unto Himself in righteousness and in faithfulness, and he who is joined unto the Lord is one spirit. Oh! marvelous mystery! We look into it, but who shall understand it? One with Jesus—so one with Him that the branch is not more one with the vine than we are a part of the Lord, our Saviour, and our Redeemer!" (Precept Austin Ministries; http://www.preceptaustin.org/2_peter_13-4.htm). See also notes 3-6 in chapter 17 on page 142.

Chapter 12—Going for It

1. John MacArthur in Don Whitney, *How Can I Be Sure I'm a Christian?* (Colorado Springs: NavPress, 1994), preface.

2. Kenneth S. Wuest, (1997). *Wuest's Word Studies in the Greek New Testament* (Grand Rapids: Eerdmans, 1997), 1 Timothy 6:12.

Chapter 13—Ten More Eternal Blessings

1. The terms "reign" (Greek, *basileusousin*) and "life" (Greek, *zōē*) are typically used for eternal life with Christ.

Chapter 14—Astonishing

1. R.T. Kendall, *Why Jesus Died: A Meditation on Isaiah 53* (Oxford, UK: Monarch Books, 2011), 118.

2. Text Analysis: Τετέλεσται, *Thayer's Greek-English Lexicon, Strong's Exhaustive Concordance*, and HELPS Word-Studies; http://concordances.org/greek/strongs_5055.htm. For a much fuller exposition see: Bruce Hurt, "John 19:30 Commentary," Precept Austin ministries; http://www.preceptaustin.org/john_1930_commentary.htm.

3. Jonathan Edwards, "Safety, Fullness, and Sweet Refreshment in Christ," at http://www.jonathan-edwards.org/Refreshment.html.

4. Robert N. Wilkin, "The Doctrine of Repentance in Church History"; http://bible.org/seriespage/doctrine-repentance-church-history.

5. R.T. Kendall, *Understanding Theology*, vol. 1 (Scotland: Christian Focus, 2002), 164.

Chapter 15—The Miracle of the New Birth

1. See at http://www.preach-the-gospel.com/R-C-Sproul-Quotes.htm.

2. Text Analysis: Titus 3:5 Strong's NT 342: ἀνακαινώσεως, *Thayer's Greek-English Lexicon*; http://concordances.org/thayers/342.htm.

3. R.T. Kendall, *Why Jesus Died: A Meditation on Isaiah 53* (Oxford, UK: Monarch Books, 2011), 179.

4. J.I. Packer, *Knowing God* (Downers Grove, IL: InterVarsity, 1993), 278.

5. Warfield's *Perfectionism* heavily critiqued Charles Finney; see Philip R. Johnson, "A Wolf in Sheep's Clothing: How Charles Finney's Theology Ravaged the Evangelical Movement"; http://www.spurgeon.org/~phil/articles/finney.htm, in which Finney is classified as heretical. Finney rejected justification by faith alone, original sin (the imputation of Adam's sin), and the vicarious substitutionary nature of Christ's atonement. Noting that modern editions of his works have been redacted and sanitized he recommends the unabridged complete and newly expanded 1878 edition of *Finney's Systematic Theology* (Minneapolis, MN: Bethany House, 1976), which "shows the real character of Finney's doctrine" and is available online at The Gospel Truth: http://www.gospeltruth.net/1851Sys_Theo/index1851st.htm.

    Defenses of Finney in critiquing Warfield tend to miss the mark, For example, see the undated "Critical Review of B.B. Warfield's 'Perfectionism: The Theology of Charles G. Finney'" by Bill Nicely, which unfortunately neglects to mention which edition of Finney's works it is quoting: http://www.pinpointevangelism.com/libraryoftheologycom/writings/moralgovernment/DefenseOfCharlesFinneysTheology-BillNicely.pdf.

    Any alleged "complete righteousness" must always be adjusted to "fluctuating ability" and so few adherents claimed 100 percent sinless perfection, but as Johnson observes there is always consequence to bad theology:

    > Finney's spiritual heirs lapsed into apostasy, Socinianism, mere moralism, cultlike perfectionism, and other related errors. In short, Finney's chief legacy was confusion and doctrinal compromise. Evangelical Christianity virtually disappeared from western New York in Finney's own lifetime…Despite Finney's accounts of glorious "revivals," most of the vast region of New England where he held his revival campaigns fell into a permanent spiritual coldness during Finney's lifetime and more than a hundred years later still has not emerged from that malaise. This is directly owing to the influence of Finney and others who were simultaneously promoting similar ideas. The Western half of New York became known as "the burnt-over district," because of the negative effects of the revivalist movement that culminated in Finney's work there.

    Apparently, despite all the revivals, few were genuine converts because this was a manmade system of theology not dependent upon the Holy Spirit. Incidentally, Warfield's *Biblical and Theological Studies* is excellent.

6. Cited in Sam Storms, *Pleasures Evermore* (Colorado Springs: NavPress, 2000), 159-60.

7. Baxter is quoted similarly in Appendix 1 of John MacArthur, *The Glory of Heaven* (Wheaton, IL: Crossway, 1996), 183: When he refers to final deliverance at the point of death from "your hard heart, those vile thoughts that lay down and rose up with you, which accompanied you to every duty, which you could no more leave behind you than you

could leave yourself behind, shall now be left behind forever. They might accompany you to death, but they cannot proceed a step further." In 1720 Thomas Boston referred to Christians in heaven being "absolute masters over sin, which had the dominion over them" (Ibid., Appendix 2, 198). MacArthur refers to the sin that "severely troubles" us believers "all our lives" and that (having spoken of Lazarus' resurrection) "the flesh constricts and fetters us, like tightly-bound grave clothes on someone just up out of the tomb" (Ibid., 121).

Chapter 16—The Miracle of Our Eternal Union with Christ

1. Erwin W. Lutzer, *How You Can Be Sure That You Will Spend Eternity with God* (Chicago: Moody, 1996), 98.

2. And by extension, given the doctrine of mutual indwelling, the Trinity itself.

3. A good brief summary article is by Jay Wegter, "Union with Christ," Frontline Ministries: "Taking Every Thought Captive: Facets of Salvation"; http://www.frontlinemin .org/union1.asp.

4. "[Union with Christ] is the cause of all other graces that we are made partakers of; they are all communicated unto us by virtue of our union with Christ. Hence is our adoption, our justification, our sanctification, our fruitfulness, our perseverance, our resurrection, our glory." John Owen at http://philgons.com/resources/bible/bibliographies/ union-with-christ/.

5. In the words of J.V. Fesco, academic dean and associate professor of systematic and historical theology, Westminster Seminary, California: "John Owen on Union with Christ and Justification"; http://thegospelcoalition.org/themelios/article/john_owen_on _union_with_christ_and_justification.

6. Bibliographies on the doctrine can be found at Dr. Phil Gons' blog and website: "Union with Christ" http://philgons.com/resources/bible/bibliographies/union-with-christ/. See also note 12 in chapter 17 on p. 143) as well as at http://www.christinyou.net/pages/union biblio.html.

7. C.S. Lewis, *Mere Christianity* (New York: Macmillan, 1977), 153.

8. Jonathan Edwards, "Safety, Fullness, and Sweet Refreshment in Christ," at http://www .jonathan-edwards.org/Refreshment.html.

9. Ibid.

10. In Keith A. Mathison, "God's Means of Assurance" in Burk Parsons (ed.), *Assured by God: Living in the Fullness of God's Grace* (Phillipsburg, NJ: P&R Publishing, 2007), 142, citing John Calvin, "Short Treatise on the Lord's Supper," in *Treatises on the Sacraments* (Fern, UK: Christian Focus, 2002), 165.

11. R.T. Kendall, *Understanding Theology*, vol. 1 (Scotland: Christian Focus, 2002), 162.

12. More is involved than an organic union; there is also the decision to abide in Christ. But note that in the previous verse Jesus teaches, "because I live, you also will live...you are in me, and I am in you." And, "We [the Father and the Son] will come to them [believers] and make our home with them" (John 14:19-20,23). He had previously encouraged the disciples to "believe me when I say that I am in the Father and the Father is in me" (John 14:11). He also referred to the fact that the Holy Spirit "will be in you" (John 14:17). In John 14:20 he taught, "On that day [after Christ's resurrection] you will realize that I am in my Father, and *you are in me*, and I am in you." The connecting of the organic unity or mutual indwelling of the Father and the Son and the believer and the Son seems inescapable.

Chapter 17—The Miracle of Our Eternal Adoption into God's Family

1. R.T. Kendall, *Understanding Theology*, vol. 1 (Scotland: Christian Focus, 2002), 162.

2. R.C. Sproul, *Chosen by God* (Wheaton, IL: Tyndale House, 1986), 137.

3. Erwin W. Lutzer, *How You Can Be Sure That You Will Spend Eternity with God* (Chicago: Moody, 1996), 94.

Chapter 18—The Miracle of Our Eternal Justification

1. Biblically, the doctrine of justification finds its roots in the Old Testament in Abel (Hebrews 11:4); Noah (Hebrews 11:7); Abraham (Romans 4:3,22-24; Galatians 3:6); King David (Romans 4:6-12); and Habakkuk (Habakkuk 2:4); and in every Old Testament passage that implies the New Covenant—e.g., Jeremiah 31; Romans 1:1-3; 3:21-22; 9:25-26. Appropriately, in Old Testament prophecy, the name by which the Messiah Himself would be known is "the LORD our righteousness" (Jeremiah 23:6 NKJV).

2. Excerpted and revised from the authors' *Protestants and Catholics: Do They Now Agree?* eBook (see http://www.amazon.com/Protestants-Catholics-They-Agree-ebook/dp/B004I43O5C/ref=sr_1_1?s=digital-text&ie=UTF8&qid=1356631098&sr=1-1&keywords=Protestants+and+Catholics%3A+Do+They+Now+Agree%3F).

3. R.T. Kendall, *Understanding Theology*, vol. 2 (Scotland: Christian Focus, 2002), 126. Its eternal nature is based in part on the fact that believers are elect and "chosen in Him from before the creation of the world"—justification logically has an eternal aspect to it. "He chose us in him before the creation of the world to be holy and blameless in his sight. In love he predestined us for adoption to sonship through Jesus Christ, in accordance with his pleasure and will—to the praise of his glorious grace...In him we were also chosen, having been predestined according to the plan of him who works out everything in conformity with the purpose of his will" (Ephesians 1:4-6,11).

4. Erwin W. Lutzer, *How You Can Be Sure That You Will Spend Eternity with God* (Chicago: Moody, 1996), 95, 98. As the great theologian John Gill asserts, "Justification is not only before faith, but it is from eternity, being an immanent act in the divine mind, and so an internal and eternal one" (John Gill, "Justification as an Eternal and Immanent Act of God"; http://www.pristinegrace.org/media.php?id=354). He continues,

> From eternal election: the objects of justification are God's elect; "Who shall lay anything to the charge of God's elect? It is God that justifies"; that is, the elect. Now if God's elect, as such, can have nothing laid to their charge; but are by God acquitted, discharged, and justified; and if they bore this character of elect from eternity, or were chosen in Christ before the world began; then they must be acquitted, discharged and justified so early, so as nothing could be laid to their charge: besides, by electing grace men were put into Christ, and were considered as in Him before the foundation of the world; and if they were considered as in Him, they must be considered as righteous or unrighteous; not surely as unrighteous, unjustified, and in a state of condemnation; for "there is no condemnation to them which are in Christ," Ro 8:1 and therefore must be considered as righteous, and so justified...(Ibid.).

This is why John Calvin, in one respect, also spoke of the eternal justification of the believer: "God did, from all eternity, decree to justify all the elect, and Christ did, in the fullness of time, die for their sins, and rise again for their justification: nevertheless, they are not justified, until the Holy Spirit doth, in due time, actually apply Christ unto them." Cited in "Eternal Justification"; http://www.theopedia.com/Eternal_justification.

Likewise the great seventeenth-century theologian Francis Turretin said, "The will or decree to justify certain persons is indeed eternal and precedes faith itself, but actual [applied] justification takes place in time and follows faith." Ibid., citing Francis Turretin, *Institutes of Elenctic Theology*, 2:683. Technically, justification is legally applied and occurs simultaneously with faith.

5. R.T. Kendall, *Why Jesus Died: a Meditation on Isaiah 53* (Oxford, UK: Monarch Books, 2011), 122.

6. Pope John Paul II, *Crossing the Threshold of Hope* (New York: Alfred A. Knopf, 1995), 194, emphasis added.

7. Greek *dikaio*; standard Greek dictionaries define the Greek word translated "justification" as an imputed, not actual righteousness: *The Hebrew-Greek Key Study Bible* (Chattanooga, TN: AMG Publishers, 1984), 23: "to render just or innocent"; Arndt and Gingrich's *Greek-English Lexicon of the New Testament* (Chicago: University of Chicago Press, 1967), 196: "being acquitted, be pronounced and treated as righteous"; *New Thayers Greek-English Lexicon* (Nappanee, IN: Evangel Publishing House, 1977), 150: "which never means to make worthy, but to judge worthy, to declare worthy, to declare guiltless, to judge, declare, pronounce righteous and therefore acceptable"; Louw and Nida's *Greek-English Lexicon* (New York: United Bible Societies, 1988), 557: "the act of clearing someone of transgression—'to acquit, to set free, to remove guilt, acquittal'"; W.E. Vine, *An Expository Dictionary of New Testament Words* (Chicago: Revell, 1966), 285: "*dikaioo*—to declare to be righteous, to pronounce righteous, being the legal and formal acquittal from guilt by God as Judge, the pronouncement of the sinner as righteous, who believes on the Lord Jesus Christ."

8. Kendall, *Why Jesus Died*, 172.

9. Sinclair Ferguson, "Assurance Justified" in Burk Parsons (ed.), *Assured by God: Living in the Fullness of God's Grace* (Phillipsburg, NJ: P&R Publishing, 2007), 91, emphasis added.

10. Ibid., 91.

Chapter 19—Accept, Cherish, and Relish God's Love for You

1. Lewis Sperry Chafer, "Assurance of Salvation"; http://www.wholesomewords.org/etexts/chafer/chaassur.html.

2. Yes, the verse goes on to say that they have been revealed in the gospel and God's promises, but the fact remains—as finite beings, we still have no idea, no conception, of what God has in store for us throughout eternity given who we are in Christ.

3. James Smith, *The Love of Christ! The Fullness, Freeness, and Immutability of the Savior's Grace Displayed!*, originally published 1860; http://www.amazon.com/Fullness-Freeness-Immutability-Displayed-ebook/dp/B008ZGNIQY.

4. For a brief study see Jay Adams, *The Grand Demonstration* (Stanley, NC: Timeless Texts, 2003).

Chapter 20—What Will Heaven Be Like? Part 1

1. Citation is given on the back cover of Jonathan Edwards, *Heaven: A World of Love* (Carlisle, PA: Banner of Truth, 2008).

2. For examples, see Don Richardson in *Eternity in Their Hearts* (Ventura, CA: Regal, 2006), and Barry Morrow, *Heaven Observed* (Colorado Springs: NavPress, 2001).

3. Colleen McDannell, Bernard Lang, *Heaven: A History* (New Haven, CT: Yale University Press, 2001), 1.

4. In terms of accurately interpreting God's Word, we are told to pay special attention to this in presenting ourselves as being approved to God because teachers of Scripture will incur a stricter judgment (James 3:1). Various translations render the original Greek word in 2 Timothy 2:15 *spoudason* (σπούδασον), by "do your best to," "work hard," "be diligent to," "study," "carefully study," "earnestly seek," give diligence to," and "strive diligently."

   Of course, if we are to meditate on heaven, how much more should we meditate on the One who occupies heaven? While the two go hand-in-glove, they can obviously be studied and meditated upon separately. Psalm 27:4 tells us that we are to "gaze on the beauty of the LORD"; Psalm 63:6 tells us we are to meditate on God "through the watches of the night"; and Hebrews 12:2-3 commands us to "fix our eyes on Jesus...consider him." Psalm 1:1-2 says we are to "delight" in and "meditate" on God's Word "day and night." As for the works of God, which include everything from Genesis to Revelation and everything in between in all creation, "Great are the works of the LORD; they are pondered by all who delight in them" (Psalm 111:2).

5. Note that in Hosea 4 the "lack of knowledge" refers specifically to the lack of the knowledge of God—i.e., theology, which is the biblical study of God. Similarly, apologetics and Christian evidences are the defense of the truthfulness of biblical teaching and the Christian worldview, which by definition includes heaven, a subject attacked (belittled and distorted) as frequently as almost anything else Christian, something that virtually has to be satanic. Being tossed out of heaven for his utterly inexcusable ungratefulness and arrogance or overbearing pride, the devil hates heaven almost as much as he hates God, something clearly reflected in both the world and much of the church's view of heaven. On the other hand, the fact that Randy Alcorn's books alone have sold more than 7 million copies is reason for hope.

6. Randy Alcorn, *Heaven* (Wheaton, IL: Tyndale House, 2006), 21.

7. A.W. Tozer, cited in Randy Alcorn, *Eternal Perspectives: A Collection of Quotations on Heaven, the New Earth, and Life After Death* (Wheaton, IL: Tyndale House, 2012), 316. Alcorn's book cites some of the best Christian scholars and writers over the last 2000 years: Augustine, Thomas Aquinas, John Calvin, Martin Luther, John Bunyan, D.L. Moody, John Newton, C.H. Spurgeon, Jonathan Edwards, John Wesley, J.R.R. Tolkien, C.S. Lewis, etc.

8. John Piper, "I AM WHO I AM," Commentary on Exodus 3:13-15, September 8, 2012, DesiringGod.org; http://www.desiringgod.org/resource-library/sermons/i-am-who-i-am—2.

9. Amy Plantinga Pauw, *The Supreme Harmony of All: The Trinitarian Theology of Jonathan Edwards* (Grand Rapids: Eerdmans, 2002), 180-81.

10. Especially since we never deserved it and we understand untold millions are suffering eternal torment in hell, something we deserved and were spared solely because of God's grace. Nor will the redeemed in heaven be at all unhappy about the fate or eternal sufferings of those in hell. We will then fully understand how evil sin truly is and how perfectly just, fair, and loving hell also truly is (so much so that we will accept it and honor it unreservedly—as even those in hell will). Further, the people in hell, even those once closest to us, will not all be perceived as those individuals we once knew; they will be as different to us as strangers because they will be seen for who they truly are. In fact, we will probably see those in hell just as the angels see their fallen brethren in hell, the very demons they are now fiercely battling behind the scenes (cf. Revelation 14:10); further, our being spared such a fate will bring us unspeakable joy forever at the mercy of God toward us.

11. Alcorn, *Heaven*, 179.

12. Sam Storms, "Heaven: The Eternal Increase of Joy" May 1, 2007; http://www.billygraham
    .org/articlepage.asp?ArticleID=810.

13. Ibid.

Chapter 21—What Will Heaven Be Like? Part 2

1. Jonathan Edwards, *Heaven, a World of Love*, at http://www.biblebb.com/files/edwards/
   charity16.htm.

2. Ibid.

3. Ibid.

4. Yes, the verse goes on to say that they have been revealed in the gospel and God's promises,
   but the fact remains, as finite beings, we still have no idea, no conception, of what God
   has in store for us throughout eternity, given who we are "in Christ." Given the length
   of eternity and the infinite triune nature of God, we never will; at best we will have hints.

5. Randy Alcorn, *Heaven* (Wheaton, IL: Tyndale House, 2006), 179.

6. Ibid., 177, emphasis in original.

7. Randy Alcorn, *Touch Points Heaven*, cited in Alcorn, *Eternal Perspectives* (Wheaton, IL:
   Tyndale House, 2012), 448-49.